Alchemical introduction
through the middle way

ISBN : 978-2-4935-7716-0
© Éditions Philomène Alchimie - 2017
27 rue de Locquirec
29620 Lanmeur - France
Site : www.editionsphilomenealchimie.com
E-mail : philomene.alchimie@orange.fr

Any reproduction, even partial, of this work is
prohibited without the permission of the author
All rights reserved, in all countries

Philomène
Philosopher by fire

Alchemical introduction
through the middle way

To Henry Coton-Alvart, whom, along with his knowledge and humility, transmitted to us the two lights with his writtings.

To Henri La Croix Haute who knew how pursuing his work and taking us with the crossroads of poetry.

Special thanks to Voyageur who could confirm the materials and provide certainty, To G. who will recognise herself and who knew how to provide the magic word, dear to Nicolas Léméry.

To each and everyone, for the tradition to continue whith humility, sincerity and impeccability.

Inside the spirit – Voyageur (traveler).

Foreword by Voyageur

« There is no use to support alchemical students in experiences that you know to be useless, as harvesting the dew or working on various salt or copper, lead or else. This can be very dangerous for their health and will lead them to nowhere.

The middle way won't allow any sidetrack, as it will be the one that let you see (if God is kind enough), in the distance, the first step of the Wise's stairway. There are 7 billion people on earth, but each and everyone has his own path, which with luck or God's gift, will allow them to have access to knowledge.

The Alchemy is a way, difficult yes, but so fulfilling as it let you understand what you, and everything around you, will become. But, if you want to know if you're on the right path, you need to rely on the full understanding of what surrounds you. If you could see the universe entirely, thanks to measuring instruments or else, you would only see three kingdoms : mineral, vegetal and animal ; and if a thought or a thinking makes you hatch, you must recognize it in everything that surrounds you.

As an example, in order to be more specific and prevent offending neophytes (as we like to call them), I can assure you that the Universe, as we percieve it, is only ebb and flow. Well ! Now we have to confirm this assertion with the observation of everything around us. In the mineral kingdom, don't we have this ebb and flow from the sea, as for the telluric energy ? In the vegetal kingdom, don't we have the ebb and flow of the sap, which enables the life of the tree ? I am sure that, for the animal kingdom, you will understand that the stop of this beat will lead you from life to death.

Alchemical introduction through the middle way

Everything below is as everything above. It's easier to understand what is below, as it is closer to us and it help us to understand the above. But first we need to let go on our beliefs, rooted in us by our education since childhood. That's why we have to understand that in life, for those who set themselves on the *royal path*, it's better to never have learned than having to unlearn. Embracing the quest of the philosopher stone, which is only a testimony of our spiritual progress, is hard. There is no buttering up in here because the work is difficult, and as is it to let go and be able to see and not to watch. Seeing is sinking in the spirit of everthing around you.

Isn't the philosopher stone a channeling of the universal spirit leading this world, in a pure and unstained matter, in order to let this spirit, after a few handlings (*easy as a child's play and women's work*) be stabilized in a suitable matter wich allows it to be seen ?

The matter is emptiness, the light is fullness and it is precisely the purpose of the Alchemist to materialize that, with of course, God's (or whatever you call him) approuval. Then arises the understanding of the Universe, of your future, of God – who isn't up there on a cloud saying "You, to the right. You, to the left" depending on the life you're living ; as He is pure love and unable to judge you. You're the only judge of your life but, for that, you'll have to live the *little death* because you can lie to God, to your friends or to your relatives but you cannot lie to yourself. It is, obviously, difficult, but the Alchemy is the work of St Thomas, and I can asssure to every newbee, that, in order to become an « I am », instead of a « Me, I » there are no path harder than this one.

So, dear friends, you are holding the story of a begining on the Alchemical way that I think usefull to every craftsman who wish to

Alchemical introduction through the middle way

get the stone and who might lead himself in pitfalls activities. If I may, here is what I wish to hear from you about seekers lost in salts and other matters equally harmfull. The work is made for the littles and to perfect it you need only a few means. Two matters are enough : one possesses the light, i.e. the sulfur, and the other one possesses the ability to expose it, i.e. the mercury. The salt is only the steam that allows their gathering.

So, dear future practictioners, here is the begining of a chat on the middle way, the one that leads on the understanding of the 'I am' and allows you to free yourself from what you already know. May God witness my words, which are in the path of honesty : this is only the begining of a conversation. You want a sequel ? That is up to you.

I am, so you know, amazingly lucky because God granted me the honor of knowing the true lineage, in France, of the adepts: Fulcanelli, who was Pierre Dujols de Valois, and taught to Henri Coton-Alvart, who taught to Henri La Croix Haute, and whom, succesively managed the making of the philosopher stone. And, myself, as an alchemist, was lucky enough to be acquainted with them and, of course, saw the Stone and all its powers.

Let yourself be lulled by the classical authors.

Voyageur

The names of the characters will be hidden in order to protect their peacefulness. As there is, for them, no reason to appear, the message always override the messenger. The rest is in the story.

From Hugo Herman (1588-1629) Pia Dessideria emblematis
« *The penitent on the path need to become aware in order to move forward* »

Introduction

« Since time immemorial, mankind has a thirst of knowledge. We seek a reason for our existence, for our being and for our future. »

This is a way, in a short, straight sentence, to introduce the questions that every people in a quest of enlightment are asking to themselves. This book aims to be a first answer by describing a short piece of the path on the journey of awarness. It is also the story of an encounter, of a conversation with a being of light, who will speak some truth with humblness in this misleaded world. Day after day, the words will connect : to the tree, to the mother earth, to the *Prima Materia,* or quite simply, to the mankind. This is a testimony that, we hope so, will bring awareness to the reader about the magic that is around us. We hope that you will find some answers that could change your everyday life and let you move forward on your own path.

Over time, the encounters we made build our road and brighten our mazes. Without the sun a flower cannot blossom, without bees it cannot expand. It is the same for the men without spirituality.

When he was 5, Mikaël was already watching where he stepped, randomly picking some peculiars rocks and fossils up from the roadsides. During the holidays in the Finistère[1], by the ocean, he was scanning every rock from the beach and collecting those who looked amazing. He started to wonder about those first encouter with the reality of the microcosm. Quickly after, he began studying some philosophers and writers : Voltaire, Rousseau, Plato, Aristote, Pascal. He loved borrowing at the Library the most ancient books, with the smell of old faded leather, enlighting readings, sometimes impenetrable. Those readings led him to more questions than answers but always brought a lot of hapiness.

Later, at 13, haunting tirelessly the Museum of Natural History, Mickäel chatted with other children, but those were taller than him, and wore wide white beards. Those old men, who spoke latin easily, accepted him gladly at their meetings in the museum. They even often took him in the fields and the woods to look up for rare flowers, herbs or mushrooms. Despite the age gap, Mikaël beeing the youngest of this guild, the complicity was real and strong between them during those Sunday getaways. A few years later, other readings – in particular the books of Gaston Rebuffat[a] and Norbert Casteret[b] narrating their adventures in the mountains or their underground explorations - gave him the desire to move foreward, higher or deeper whithin the earth. He needed to get off the books to

---

[1] *Traductor's note* : Region from the west of France, in Bretagne.
[a] Gaston Rebuffat, 1921-1985, french alpinist and writer. He opened new climbing routes, wich are now legendary. Member of the Annapurna expedition in 1950.
[b] Norbert Casteret, 1897-1987, french speleologist and writer, discovers in 1922 the oldest statues of the world, in the cavern of Montespan, and in 1931, on the spanish side of the Pyrenees, the true spring of the Garonne River.

satisfy his thirst for adventure and start to find answers for his teenage questions. So, during abroad adventures the challenges he shared with rope mates taught him the depth, the reality of his intimacy with the earth, water, air and fire. The long waiting in the cold, under frozen waterfalls or the brotherhood experienced in the sharing of a light meal, allowed him to live true and straightforward encounters.

After years of joyfull, and sometimes challenging quest, every day, every encounter began, for him, unique times when he needed to BE fully to fully be.

This is how, by following his quest, Mikaël met his future wife Pernelle during an underground exploration. They both devoted themselves to the exploration of a lot of churches, cathedrals and ancient buildings. They become passionate about the stained-glass windows and old stones, and wondered about their chemical content, about the meaning of the painted or carved symbols.

Mikaël wondered if all this could have another meaning than the one showed to the commonplace. Was it only ornamental beauty or could there be hidden messages ? Were only common stories told there or could there be hidden secrets ? They found, everytime, the same patterns, so the poor explanations written on the churches fold gave us a bitter taste, a feeling of emptiness and a scent of unsolved mystery. There must be an hidden meaning, but wich one ?

During their exploration, Mikaël and Pernelle took an impressive amount of pictures, by all weather and until their neck and back hurted. Nothing could stop them, it became compulsive, again and again, for hours, scanning the canopies, the pillars, the ceilings, the porches.

Everything was scruted, and, once they got back home, the addiction continued with the enlargment of the pictures and the analysis of some details that could have been unnoticed.

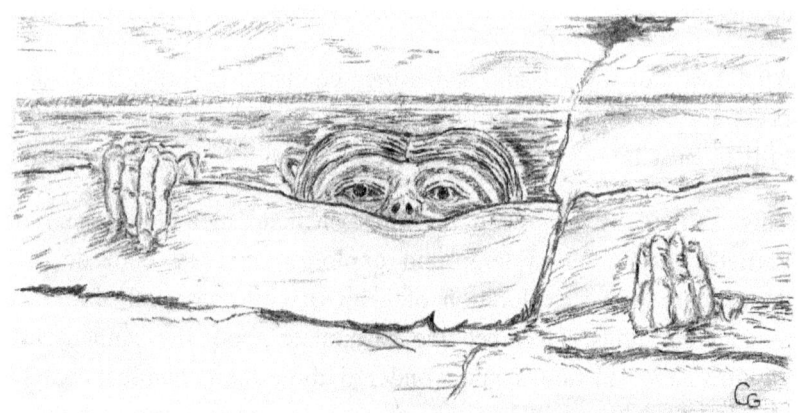

The nosy of Conques in Aveyron, France.

All this work didn't brought much more clarity but gave a meaning, a logical follow-up, as a necessary step towards a common thread that would lead to a new form of consciousness

After a few years, and tens of thousands of pictures, they couldn't miss any layman detail. Mikaël could spot similarities between sculptures and stained-glass windows of all the buildings. But damn ! How to find the sacred meaning, hidden from the eyes of the layman ? He could feel the existence of the magic and the wonderful here, reachable, slightly veiled but something was missing to make the first step towards the knowledge.

Alchemical introduction through the middle way

Glad about his discoveries, Mikaël published his pictures and wondering on the social media. He wanted to offer, to give the desire to go exploring those buildings, sharing was his key word, his leitmotiv. That is how he made wonderfull encounters on the internet, wich sometimes leaded to real life meetings. There were many, as he was, exploring, photographing and seeking. One of them, who became later a friend, was talking with him about symbolism. One day occured when, in order to go deeper, in a confidence, a word was said : Alchemy. With its three principles : the salt, the sulfur and the Mercury[1], the three Kingdoms : mineral, vegetal, animal... A number that kept coming back : the THREE !

Then Mikaël took the time to read the books that his friend advised him to read : « *The Mystery of the Cathedrals* », from a certain Fulcanelli[2], « *The Two Lights* » from Henri Coton-Alvart[3], «L'Or du millième matin» [c] from Armand Barbault[4], ...

The stories were beautiful, the character mysterious but all this didn't gave any new understanding, in fact it was quite the opposit, the messages painted on the stained glass or the sculptures on the cathedrals became more obscure.

Since then, he needed to read again and again, work and repeat until he was able to see some connections that would lead him to a better understanding of those who, too often, would pronounce themselves philosopher as no one could contradict them. All along the History, they let some marks of their progression in the stone and the glass, providing to posterity their veiled messages, as Isis, with the seal of

---

[c] « *Gold of a thousand Mornings* »

perception. How the labytinth is long and winding ! Can we only get trough it ? Alone ? Accompanied ?

« When the student is ready, the Master appears[d] ».

Doc Faust, the one we will then be refered as the *Illuminated* follows the wandering of anonymous people on the internet, that ask themselves a lot of questions, pose and presuppose, people like Mikaël, reliable but a bit lost in those debates where surfers argue with each other in fratricidal jousting, gratifying only their mutual ego. So, with his wisdom, the initiated distills some smalls touch of light in those arguments, answering the assertions with questions. However, to Mikaël, those questions strongly seemed to be real answers. He started then to ask himslef, to question everything, to judge by himself, to not believe without any evidence. He started to make some assumption about the creation, he had the desire to ask himself, even if the answers don't get to him. Doc Faust tells him about his quest, he words some advices in order to climb the three first narrow steps which leed to the front door of the labyrinth...

A fragile bond is forged, the begining of a linkage, some exchanges are created, the discussion are surrealistic because they are so different from everything that we could already read, or see or hear. Magic works, faiths sets in, the discussion continues and a relationship is established between the one who knows and the one who wants to learn. The exchange is always made of simple words,

---

d Proverbe bouddhiste / Buddhist saying.

references to nature, myths, anecdote... as a result ideas and logics sink in. He knows that fate is sending him a sign.

Aware of the anachronism of this exchange between a person of the present and another whom he already describes as timeless, he begins to take some notes, nothing must be lost, each of the words must serve the benefit of the all so that everyone can find the message that is specific to him...

Hours and hours of chat will be collected. The spirit of these quickly reveals themself to be a true gift of knowledge, as one would pass the witness flame to a marathon runner.

This large amount of time, which is in no way wasted, appears to be the beginning of a timeless teaching. Mikaël then thinks of those who will one day read these words of truth, those who will seek to become a tiny bit better every day.

In awarness, with a little help, but on your own, you can start learning and understanding the world around you with respect and humbleness.

*

So, this is what the surveyor of Space and Time said to the pilgrim.

The beginning of the teaching

Ancient engraving - Pilgrimage Museum in Santiago de Compostela

Since the begining, the exchanges between Mikaël and Doc Faust were very bright. Mikaël does not yet realize that what follows will change his destiny...

Alchemical introduction through the middle way

Doc Faust : The challenge of the transmission of knowledge is, above all, to have in front of you experts in everything and especially in our craft, who, given their certainties, will or will not have the strength of character to unlearn. A real miracle if it happens. And yet, how could we fill of water a glass that is already full ? Let's start by emptying the tank in order to fill it up.

We are like in the story of "Hop O' My Thumb"[e], the one who pushes and who knows throws little white stones in the form of allegories, questions, sometimes even suggesting answers. Maintaining a dialogue and questioning is already giving knowledge. The difficulty in a relationship is the time that can be devoted to it to make it fruitfull and enjoyable. This explains why that there are many called but few chosen. The aspirant will engage in a faith trial where he only must behave. It's like entering into religion without coming back. It is a path of efforts and sacrifices with five moral principles that will have to be cultivated throughout the path. These values are expressed in five words : respect, humbleness, propriety, uprightness, truth.

The issue in a spiritual ambition, and even more so if alchemical, is to adjust a quest for the wonders, the incredible, the unlikely that will transcend the artist's daily life and his daily routine. A kind of mind split where the two aspects of life will have to coexist without making us loose our minds. Thus, we will percieve by ourselves what is common from what is universal, as we can find in the verbs

---

[e] In French "le petit poucet" – the small/young pusher

to feel or to be. Alchemy is timeless and universal, it is implemented by Mother Nature.

The understanding is done according to his own knowledge, and transforms a ME I into I AM because from the nothing we will make a Whole. The universal coexists with the common man in his everyday life, it illuminates the book of life of the one who will be able to open his soul and heart. The alchemist is a gardener who will grow in his chaos the three roses : knowledge, understanding and compassion.

Mikaël : Yes, indeed, everything is Alchemy, without knowing it, we always perceive it, it seems essential to me to be a daily spiritual enrichment. To be on the right track, it is necessary to move away from the "pseudo-mysteries" and ancillary topics. They are probably interesting, but it is a waste of time and energy that distracts us from the main purpose. The various amazing subjects disturb the journey because if time is undefined for nature, it is counted for man. From this arises alchemy : chemistry with a slight touch of the Spirit from above, a craft that uses philosophy as a way of introspection and science as means of action. Alchemy replicates to the human dimension what nature does without time pressure[f] and on a larger scale.

Doc Faust : The issue of the layman is that he believes, through his readings or through the people he listens to, that he understands the

---

[f] An ancient chinese saying sums up the temporality of men in front on the eternal nature « The beef is slow but nature is patient ».

whole of a thousands years old science. At most, he can capture a piece of light, but he first would have to perceive it inside him. But an Adept does not write or speak to make himself understood, he writes to testify about what he is, what he has done, his state of being or - rarely- to deliver a message. So, we don't move forward in alchemy by reading but, as it is said, by burning our books to finally start thinking and working. Being helped does not consist in receiving answers but in bearing questions that, through thinking, will make you progress on your own.

The Adepthood

Based on a mural fresco of the church of Saint André d'Alet-les-bains

Adept comes from the Latin "adeptus" or "the one who has attained", but to be closer to our philosophy, we will say "the one who received". In alchemy, the adept is the one who has reached the Great Work and fulfilment by becoming a receptacle of divine light...

Alchemical introduction through the middle way

Mikaël : First of all, can you explain to me what an Adept his, and how we become one ?

Doc Faust : It's a vast question, and my definition depends on the context, the time, the place where it is asked and especially the people listening. At first, the adept is for me the one who is in favour of... And we'll see later that interpretation can quickly become more complex as we walk on the frontiers of science debate on quantum physics where space and time are playing tricks even to the most intelligent.

But let's start by making it simple, let's take the master's limit and position ourselves at the level of the language relationship between two men. I would say that we cannot declare ourselves adepts or that would no longer make us a « light master »[g], but a chalk transfer. The peers give you the title, sometimes after your death, because humbleness towards your Creator, who covers you with his blessings, forbid you to proclaim yourself with this pompous title. You'll never hear me say : I'm an Adept. Besides... It doesnt' matter, I'm not enlisting or selling a book. About that, allow me here to say my will, in accordance with my beliefs : the profits from the sale of this book will be donated to a good cause (which is certainly not mine). We are writing out of charity and not out of interest.

---

[g] The term "master" will often be replaced in this book by "enlightened", wich is more appropriate as in the Western countries « master » applies rather to the teacher, the one who has science, who speaks while the student is silent. You have to be the student of yourself because there is more to learn as a student than as a teacher. And thus the student rises.

However, I feel that you are frustrated so I will give you one of the view that we could have of the Adept : he may be a person initiated according to the tradition. It means, being initiated by a person who has already watched the miraculous effects of our art. Then the candidate will have to devote himself to the only true way, the one called the *pathway* wich is enough by itself to see the most beautiful treasures of nature.

To this day, this way seems to me to be the only praticable one to receive the light of the Creator. The finisher on the middle way (an other term for the royal way) will have received his knowledge from another Adept, wich is, by the way, really uncommon indeed, because lots them are self-proclaiming, but few really are.

The light of the other one can be seen through the lenght of the talks, wich never contradict themselves, while remaining under the seal of sacred.

Besides, Henri Coton-Alvart said that the West only forged a handful of Adept by centuries.

But let's go back to the ethicals standarts required to let you become a potential recipient. The Adepthood is a state of being, based on humbleness and compassion combined with the knowledge of the laws that govern the light forces, which are interacting in the universal whole. Like stillness in vastness.

But I wish to no one to own such a knowledge, because there is a price to pay. The Adepts, with the speeding up of their knowledges, in return recieve the magnified shock of the universal misery, that is why they avoid to be seen and isolate themselves from this world effervescence, even though they are present to it they try to not bear it all.

The Adept is a person who, all the way through is rising, has prepared himself to keep his humbleness with the increasing of his knowledges and his powers. It is someone who purifies his own matter and who receive in exchange the means of his one purification, until one day, becoming enlightened from it.

For the materialists, the Adept is the one who *reorganized* the philosopher's stone and who proceeded to a transmutation. In this case, the mistake is often made to consider the person who get a materialization of the Work as legitimate to aspire to some spiritual elevation. As if the material took over the spiritual, but it isn't like that.

For others, the Adept would be the one who has absorbed the alchemical medicine, though it would be necessry to know if it is from the first, second or third order. Honestly, all of this matters only to the one who wish to flatter his ego by receiving the relative recognition from the world around him. I almost want to say : we acknowledge the Adept that we deserve.

If I had to talk about the qualities required from the Adept, I think deep down inside, that it is the one who doesn't contradict the armed arm of divine justice, who own the philosopher's stone and who made from it the testimony for himslef. It is the one who, sick, will have the wisdom to not absorb it. Finally, he is the one who think with a different state of mind, in order to connect and tune in the universe until being able to influence the matter and the spirit while stopping his view of time.

Mikaël : I read the book « *Les clés du Labora-T-ore* » *(i.e The keys of the Labora-T-Ore).* In the first pages we can find something that looks like a curse or, at least, a warning called « *Comparution* » *(i.e*

Appearance). It all seemed to me very solemn, why did they published it ?

Doc Faust : For an apprentice, it probably is the most complete text about laboratory[h] experimentation. This notebook chronicles most of the experiences when Henri Coton-Alavard worked with the complicity of P. Dujols. But this book wasn't meant to be published.

The notes of Jean-François Gibert, friend of our dear Henri Coton-Alvart, were handwritten and therefore almost indecipherable. It took a few people six months of hard work to transcribe them into a digital format that could be donated to our community, and used for the greater good. Copies of these notes were spread clandestinely at a high price by a few illegitimate and unscrupulous people. Then the free publication of these notebooks enabled to stop this dubtful practice, which harmed the alchemists' reputation. We do not trade with what God has given us by grace.

---

h This notebook is the start of the Fulcanelli's myth. From my point of view, the work allocated to Fulcanelli are a romance of the partnership between Pierre Dujols de Valois and Henri Coton-Alvart. The alias Fulcanelli can be summarized as follows: an erudite and an operative working hand by hand on a side, and on the other side a writer and illustrator in charge of restoring alchemy's pedigree by reconnecting with the legend. The most amazing is that, in this time, none of them were adepts, Henri Coton-Alvard having recieved the grace only years later, in the 70's. I'm really torn between an Eugène Canseliet who, on one hand restored the image of alchemy by giving it a new pedigree wich everyone can finally believe in, but on the other hand distorted the truth by certifying the Fulcanelli's Adepthood whereas Pierre Dujols was only using a stock of light that had been entrusted to him.

Alchemical introduction through the middle way

About « *Comparution* », it is a warning for those who wish to become guru, hosting expensive and useless courses, knowing that they own nothing of the ancient's sience and would be misleading the fellow men. By stealing your neighbour you just fool yourself. Here's all the story about that !

Why would a guru teach the very thing that makes him earn his money ? Revealing the secret would make him a mere nobody, anonymous and disoriented. But another truth appears as the reason to this publication, a bit as the warning that we can find on the front door of the parisian catacombs :

STOP – THIS IS THE DEATH EMPIRE

None of the messenger will get down in history, the message only can survive through time... I often think about this "philosopher" skull that we find in the think tank of the *widow's children* who awakes us with its whisper...

Alchemical introduction through the middle way

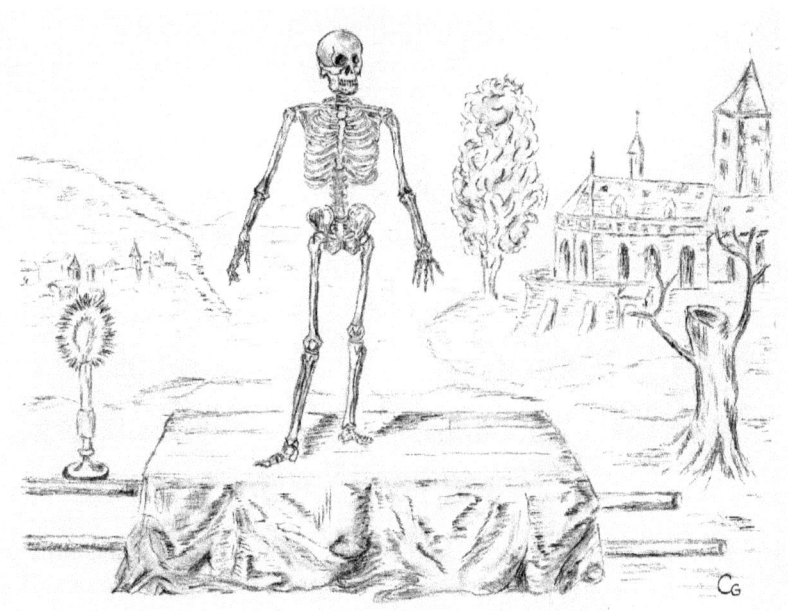

« I was what you are, I am what you will be ! »
... the messenger will have to fade in front of our creator.

Mikaël : What bothers me the most with those new prophets, who take on the legitimacy of the Ancients' words without even quoting them, it is their Relationship with the 'gift of God (*Donum Dei)*', which, as you already said, cannot be sold or bought.

And about the courses, I attented to one at the very begining, it was a first and for sure the last one, very expensive and absolutely useless !

As in " Le saut de la foi (i.e. *The leap of faith)* " where we see that, by willing too much to receive effortlessly we sink more deeper in the labyrinth's nebula.

The truth encourages us to find stillness and peace at its core while scanning all the challenges we have undergone. Because, as you so well said, the light needs the dark to be seen.

Doc Faust : How does the alchemy's wonders applies and can help you in your daily life ?

> *La*
> *La lumière*
> *La lumière a besoin*
> *La lumière a besoin de l'obscurité*
> *La lumière a besoin de l'obscurité pour*
> *La lumière a besoin de l'obscurité pour être vue*

The light needs darkness to be seen

Mikaël : Every day, since childhood, I allow myself some time to tune in with nature, flowers, stones, cristals. It is this way of living that brought me to create florals' elexirs. The spagyria[i] is based on the same principle than the alchemy : To separate and to reunite.

The extraction process of the medicinals virtues is accomplished by separating the three elements and then, after purification, by reuniting them to get an elixir. Well, actually I'm still in the learning phase because the path is tricky. So, in order to move foreward, I need the good theaching, to guide me. I know how lucky I am, to meet the right people on my way, and, above all, always at the right time.

---

[i] Spagyria: from the greek « spào et ageirô » or the art of separating and gathering the main components of the body.

Doc Faust : That is how it works. If you listen the nature helps you whith its blessings. It makes you meet at the usefull time people from various backgrounds. About the learning phase, don't worry, it is better not to know than having to unlearn. Everyone can play a character, every good teaching is based on the free gift of our knowledge and humbleness is crucial to keep the grace of God. This gift that we receive cannot, in any way, be monetized, or you loose it. One of the fist time I spoke about the gift was with my friend Bruno, a talented magnetic healer, he was provinding cares to people without asking anything in return, everyone gave an anonymous offering, depending on their means and the care they got.

The Bomarzo Gardens in Italy
"Abandon every hope, all you who enter !"
(Inferno - Dante - Source Wikipedia)

He was persuaded that, if he had trade his gift, it would have disapeared as quickly as it had be given. Thus, some, instead of sharing benefits, will sell themselves : but they are misleading. They committ the worst sin[j] against the spirit, specifically the holly spirit. They should know that it is the only irreconcilable one, it can't be forgiven either up or down. One of those unknowned Works, yet so well written, is called "Clef des œuvres de Saint Jean et Michel de Nostredame (i.e. *Keys of the Works of Saint John and Michael of Nostredame)"*. The author used the alias MA de Nantes[k] and is allegedly Aristide Monnier (1824-1899). With such a title, it seems like a perfect introduction, the theoretical and operative work being barely veiled. I give this reference because I want to give a good first book to read for those who are discouraged by their readings and wish to get off to a good start. I also think about an other text which gave our art's his pedigree back, I see it as THE founding text of the twenty century's Alchemy. It's the "Labora-T-Ore" whose we already spoke about. Henri Coton-Alvart and Pierre Dujols describe their alchemical experiences transposed from ancient texts to the laboratory. They show how to get from the speculative Alchemy to the operative one. It is a breakthrough event in alchemy's history. Those works allowed then the emergence of Fulcanelli, and then all the abuses that we know.

---

[j] Also called blasphemy againt the Holy Spirit, from a Jesus' quote common to the three synoptic gospels « Whoever has speak against the Holy Spirit, will not be forgiven, nor is this world or in the other ». (Mt, 12, 31-32)
[k] Pierre Aristide Monnier published this book in 1872 under the alias MA (Master Artist) de Nantes.

The Alchemist of Notre Dame "Straight as the mind, his gaze is not on the horizon but on his matter"

The Fulcanelli's Myth

« The strongest impression of our early youth was the emotion that the sight of a Gothic cathedral caused in our child's soul. We were immediately transported, ecstatic, unable to tear ourselves away from the attraction of the wonders... »
Mystery of the Cathedrals - Fulcanelli

Doc Faust : I often read that 'Fulcanelli' could be a man or a group of people ! What matters is that the messenger will alway fade behind the message. I prefer the idea of the group of people because it makes it easier to go further and faster, as the *Watchmen's group*[1]. did in its days. The several discussions between everyone helps to rediscover the values of sharing. Down here neither God, nor Master ; just various sensibilities working for a greater goal, more admirable than our small existence and all this, once again, in a disinterested way. A well-organized group will go much further than an individual who holds undivided authority by abusing his loyal idle sheep.

---

[1] Henri Coton-Alvart, R. Schwaller, Miloz de Lubicz, C. Larronde, G. Revel, L. AllainGuillaume, … and some others, from esotercis, artistic and literary (including P. Loti, F. Léger, C. Flammarion) joined this initiatory group advocating a new society that valued manual and artistic work, their motto was "To live to excel", work becoming a goal and not a means, money becoming a means and not a goal.

Alchemical introduction through the middle way

Mikaël : You talk about Fulcanelli, indeed, we fight over his true identity from ages... but it doesn't really matter because, according to Enguène Canseliet, he wished to remain anonymous. Looking up now to discover his identity, isnt'it going against his first will, and by then, putting his work in the background ? I read that the Adepts, after getting the stone, become *invisible*, and disapear of the civil life, we don't see or here them anymore. Is it like that for all the Adepts and why ?

Doc Faust : Eugène Canseliet (1899-1982) cloud the issue about Fulcanelli to get a bit of notoriety through this myth. Pierre Dujols de Valois (1862-1926) was initiated by the Adept Paul Decoeur (1839-1923), whom, in addition of his teaching gave him, soon before his death, a tiny supply of philosopher's stones, which he then used to make some transmutation in 1922. Pierre Dujols continued his journey with the help of Henri Coton-Alvart (1894-1988), their relationship can even be described as a Master to a disciple. When they decided to reconstitute all the notes they possessed they entrusted the writting of *'Mystery of cathedrals'* to Eugène Canseliet. He invented then, with the help of Julien Champagne (1877-1932), the alias Fulcanelli, which in the end represents not one person but an association of four individuals. An intellectual leader : Pierre Dujols, an engineer and talented operative : Henri Coton-Alvart, a writter : Eugène Canseliet and an illustrator : Julien Champagne.

But again, the identity doesn't matter, the message given to posterity does ! Fulcanelli is immortal because his book will survive through History ! Those who seek to know his true identity are often those who are lost in the maze and wish to find -with this disclosure- new clues that would help them to go further !

And there is also those apprentices who read and replicate the nonsenses written in the books, and the future puffers, and those who burn the books to start thinking from the nature's laws. I'm afraid that the modern alchemy is just a misled interpretation of the « *Labora-T-Ore* » and that, instead of arising alchemist, we are limited to creating regulus melters.

So, we encounter two kinds of apprentice, as their is two kinds of Adepts : those who were able to stay on the bright side of the force with humbleness, and those who let themselves be tempted by the dark side by trying to become icons. But once they are paid in cold hard cash, their orientation on the path becomes irreversible. You are either to the right or to the left of the creator. The warning is from the Last Judgment, written on the pediment of some cathedrals.

This warning is written in my alias *Doc Faust*, because what we should remember of this story is the man that knew how to understand the true wisdom and dispossess himself from the material to obtain his redemption, and not the man who wanted to transgress Mother Nature's laws by making a pact with the devil.

Discretion is the key word of Light's Being. They consider their knowledge as a responsability and a burden that could, if it was revealed, turn the world upside down. I knew someone on the path, who find himslef harrassed by potentials followers, ready to do anything to break into his life. The only solution he had then, was to die. We laughed a long time at this trick we played on them. Great honors are great burden. Some things and some powers cannot be revealed or the dark side would triomph.

Mikaël : I suppose that getting the Stone changes a lot of things in the erveryday life, and in the relationships with others but also with oneself. In our many discussions, I realize that you are charismatic and wise. Becoming Adept must be wonderfull, but tell me, how do you handle it on a daily basis ?

Doc Faust : The best approach is to think that our consciousness' field is changed, time is no longer valid, the moment is exalted. When the mind is mobilized during a split second, it causes a temporal tear that brings omniscience and omnipotence. Faced with a problem, we no longer look up for a solution, we immediately have it. There is a lot of similarity with Asperger's syndrome, which makes the brain work differently. And I would add an almost extra cerebral connectivity with a *beyond* that allows the immediacy of the answer to a question.

Mikaël : How many Adepts do you know ? Do you speak to each other ? It is also said that two Adepts will recognize each other even if they have never met before, is that correct ?

Doc Faust : I was born to late to meet the Adept Henri Conton-Alvart, nor his disciple Henri La Croix Haute[5]. My begining into the lineage starts with the meeting of one of the few Adept women, disciple in the tradition that I consider as the true french lineage, that some consider as Fulcanelli's... Well, their still might be some abnormalities that will be forgotten through history.

The cenacle formed in northern France and southern Belgium remains, who works discreetly, away from the media and in accordance with tradition.

In the end, the state of being of all of those honorable people coexist with other reference field, progress and understanding. Don't forget that the light we receive only magnifies what you are, good or bad, depending on our education, readings and dreams. They all have different backgrounds and interests, but again, exemplary manners and absolute discretion.

On this philosopher's path, you must always keep in mind that the good and the bad coexist, and that mankind is the incarnation of this last one. That is why, if I meet someone receptive to my teaching, I can help rising his philosophy but, in no way take responsability to create in the laboratory world destroyers[m].

Mikaël : The Rumor also says that an Adept is "shining, that his "energy" can be seen by everyone, in other words that he is different. And it is true that when I met you I saw it at first sight.

Doc Faust : The luminous state of being is real, and I am quite vigilant about it. Being seen by everyone, even if they don't *perceive* you, can be extremely dangerous depending on the "kindness" of the people encountered. Once, in India, I was wandering in a famous temple of Bombay and watching, from a distance, the offerings made to the gods (*Puja*). The believers standed during hours on the waiting line to be able to pray, bow down, give food, flowers and objects to the gods.

---

[m] « I became Death, the world destroyer » J. Robert Oppenheimer

Suddenly, an old man starts staring at me, he gently pulls me in front of the altar, joins my hands as if I was praying, then surrounds them with necklaces of flowers, and finally opens them and gives me food intented for the deities. Then he joined his hand above mine and says : "I was waiting for you, I see you, you're really lucky, gods blessed you because you're surrounded by their light." Actually, this man was the oldest and most respected priest of this temple. The faithfuls there were wondering themselves about what just happened. The old man hadn't spoke for years... And then, nothing. He left, proud of himslef and with a huge smile on his face.

Then things begins to go wrong, the moment of stillness and peace is quickly broke by an oppressive crowd that surrounds me and starts to get closer and closer, asking me questions, requesting answers... I was lucky to inspired them a kind of fear, otherwise I think that I never would have been able to quicly escape and leave the temple. So, being seen can be really dangerous and that is why don't go public very often, never on my true identity or only by creating a mental barrier to protect me. Anonymity easily allows me to pretend to be a fool for a large audience, instead of an enlightened man, which would be more dangerous.

Mikaël : Rumor also says that an Adept can be *"here and elsewhere"*, what does it means ?

Doc Faust : Once again, I can only speak for myself and from my own experience, which might continue to evolve over time. The thruth is that we learn everyday. So it is somewhat paradoxical to claim holding the truth, as it might be only a part of it. In an Adept's state two moments coexist, the original state and the enlightened one. The state of light just want to fly away to the original state. The state of the man's daily life will so join - in spirit – what some call *the God's shape* to own for a brief moment His characteristics.

The mind flying over the primordial cloud above the waters, demands to cross the limits of our traditional physics and our certainties. I would say that it looks like quantum physics but with flows endowed with consciousness and corpuscles endowed with cataclysmic powers.

The Adept is the one that goes from a macroscopic physical dimension to a quantum dissolution. In an instant, the mind is reduced to a quantum state, and, by then, possesses all its properties, and universality as well.

But playing with quanta states can be much more dangerous than a crowd of faithful in an Indian temple. If the subject abuses his power without mastering them, he can suddenly find himself dissipated in the universe – without being able to come back to is original state of being.

Mikaël : Apart from the Adepts, have you ever met people with the same spiritual evolution ?

Doc Faust : Yes, I recently encountered a *Compagnon du Devoir*[n], thanks to our long chats and convergence of mind he soon became my friend Michel. I think about the making of an alchemical artefact

---

[n] *Compagnon du devoir* is a French guild where the student tours France for his apprencticeship, in various areas : carpenters, mason, boilermaker, landscape gardener, etc. (TN)

these days and his talents of sculptor, melter, welder, engraver help me a lot. It is really strange to find in the artwork people who convey the same philosophy and values that the Adepts defend through the alchemical tradition.

This artefact will be made in the purest guild's tradition. It funny how destiny brought together two experts in distincts arts but, in the end, reunited under the banner of one philosophy, for a real joint initiation project !

The artefact will be made in wood, the tree will be cut down according to an ancestral ritual, a transmitted and not lost knowledge that only the *Companions* transmit by word of mouth. The tree will be chosen in the forest according to its location on favourable telluric tides. We're going to explain to the tree that it isn't the end of is life but a new begining, a "re-birth" in its new life. In the alchemical's philosophy, it is said that we must go through the *little death* one fisrt time to let the light shine so that we can rise again.

But, lets go back to our tree. He will be tied up, drained of his vital energy without dying, by incising the sapwood, he will gradually during two or three years- transfer his vital energy to the ground. Then, it will be the time for the *Compagnon* to work on it, and it will be reborn in its second shape. But this project isn't going to end soon, as their is so much to do around us... and so little time to spend on so many projects.

We must be silent

« To know, to will, to dare, to be silent »

"*Tacere*" is required. Words that fly in the wind are unnecessarily lost and corrupt more than they germinate
.

Alchemical introduction through the middle way

Doc Faust *:* I will say more about the work in a next book which will address more the practical aspect of operations, I will talk the consecration of the places and tools, the activation of the oratory, and then about the laboratory, the safety and dangerousness of the products and metals with their deadly impact on the health of the philistine who might not proceed properly... It is a crime to let philistines go on alchemicals ways without any training about the laboratory techniques. You can't improvise yourself an alchemist ! You become one...

Here, I will only talk about the philosophy, the state of mind, the preparation to receive, because before running you must learn how to walk. Especially since it is the pilgrim who makes the journey and not the one who accompanies him. The pilgrim must then put himself in shape. He must be in the right state of mind : Openness, Humbleness, Respect, Alignment, in order to be ready to let the light pass through him, to rectify himself, to set out on his journey seeking for the good.

Then, everyone must set a goal and work on it. We cannot walk in someone else's path, *Ore* and *Labore* (pray and work) because the two go together. Nature uses exchanges, the gift comes automatically by the positive return of the matter, if the first intentions are good.

Mikaël *:* How long have you been interested by the Ancient's sacred Art ?

Doc Faust *:* My grand mother introduced me to Alchemy at a very young age. She was a humble person, on the right side of the force, that made me see the wonders in my daily life. I was very lucky. She claims that she was the keeper of my destiny and that my arrival had been anounced to her. Then she just needed to open her eyes and wait to set my roots in the tradition.

Actually, it isn't necessary to do Alchemy to be an alchemist. We just need to open our eyes wide to watch the nature that surrounds us and be impregnated by it, everyday. With Alchemy, catching nature is feeling it and living it, as ebb and flow. You throw a stone into the pond and the concentric circles are a reflection of the founding laws of alchemy, they follow the law of propagation and evangelization.

The newborn does an alchemical miracle with his birth, and then he forgets it. The newborn child inhales and exhales as the first manifestation of his life.

Sacred symbolism's

Salvador Dalí's Vision – St George slaying the dragon

Symbolism is the basis of the "*relevant analogies, homologies, associations of ideas, connotations, relationships between the primary meaning of the symbol and the figurative meanings that allow this extraction of the symbolized meanings.* » T. Todorov

Doc Faust : The book of MA de Nantes, named "*Clef des Œuvres de Saint Jean et de Michel de Nostredame »* is going to help you because it explains clearly the Oratory. Then, in your experiment, you must use the principles, the *modus operandi* that you will be able to tame... Actually, we must connect what our senses tell us and confront it with the signs that nature sends us. It is the sum of this five senses, or quintessence, that made us distinguish the truth from the fake. An example : if you see a Lion (clawed paws) and an Eagle (spreaded wings)°, you can instantly distinguish the *Volatil* and the *Fixed*, the *Air* from the *Earth* ! You can also notice the union of the Masculine (a lion) and the feminine (an eagle), the active and the passive, the ebb and flow, the *solve* and the *coagula* (dissolve and gather), the hot and cold, the dry and the wet, ...

Nature works in a dual way by endlessly seeking to reconcile its opposites around a median point. Even if some people try, with more or less efficiency, through three elements -sulphur, salt and mercury- nature loves couples, even in a marriage, the "priest" must disappear because he has nothing to do into their the intimacy. All this is rather witty, but the only important thing is the revelation that appears in a moment of stillness, like a spark that springs from the depths of eternity.

° Saint Jerome of Stridon tells us that the four Livings (also called the Tetramorph) have an other purpose than representing the four Gospels Mark, Matthew, John and Luke. Those ones sum up four essential moments of the Christ's life. The Word of God was incarnated (Man), he was tempted in the desert (Lion), he was set on fire (bull) and ascended to heaven.

Alchemical introduction through the middle way

It is –indeed– hard to forge a new path of thought, but with work and daily effort it becomes a reflex, a feeling at every moment. At first, it's obscure, but gymnastics is done slowly.

It is the grain of sand that, from the top of the mountain, descends the slope and is finally accompanied by an avalanche of much larger stones. It is the unification of opposites by the salt of the wattered that penetrates your matter. Actually the dew is much more allegorical than we think, and the alchemist - if he understands its true meaning - will know how to make it a dewy, dawning and daring art.

Mikaël : So, Doc, when we see sculptures and stained glass windows depicting Saint Michael knocking down the dragon, isn't it a bit the same as the Lion and the Eagle, as the *Fixed* and the *Volatile* ?

Doc Faust : Yes Mikaël, we keep saying the same things but with various symbols, we seek a story in history, the meaning is often the same. For example, St George and St Michael who will put their spear or sword in a dragon's throat (to strike down and not pierce), so that a fire from above will extinguish a fire from below, this refers to the alchemical operation called "*to put the dragon in the ground*". In order to progress the apprentice will keep his child soul wide open. The *work* is easy and can be summarized up in a few dozen of operations. Well, without mockery, a twelve-year-old child would be able to make the philosopher's stone : isn't it said in the *Aureum* *vellus*[p] or later in the Splendor Solis[q], that the whole alchemical work is summed up as a woman's work and a child's play ?

However, mastering the whole alchemical operations requires many years of hard work and perseverance. The child should be accompanied by a good chemistry teacher for obvious safety concerns. We beware of fumes, but the vapors are even more toxic because they are invisible and the reactions are surprising and countless. It would be criminal to encourage an inexperienced audience to work with materials such as antimony, cinnabar and other poisons. A qualified chemistry teacher cannot consciously let a student poison himself without being personally responsible here and to God.

Mickaël : Yes, and that is exactly the issue, to control your mind, to keep a part of your child's soul, not to burden yourself in life with too many useless books, not to pollute yourself with the acts of your past, simply to be in the moment, now. Live the magical moment, like on trips in the high mountains, or underground.

Inside the earth, you are as if you were in the matrix, you are fine there, sometimes in spite of the death that borders you, during endless waiting in a cramped gut or even too long stowed in the rock face to a simple piece of metal in a wild and free nature. In these moments, you feel the presence of the divine, it is omnipresent. You

---

[p] *Aureum velus* or Golden Fleece, work of Salomon Trismosin 1568.
[q] The *Splendor Solis* is an handwritten alchemical treatise from the 16th century, written in German, and famous for its series of coloured illustrations.

are then in balance, straddling a spark of eternity that has stopped the time around you. Man is a wisp of straw faced with the sudden rage of nature that could arise.

Doc Faust : As we progress along the path, the goal moves away, at least in appearance. We become more aware of the small size of the pilgrim and his narrow-mindedness in the face of the path that remains to be travelled...

Everyone has their own way, with their own set of unlikely encounters on the paths of the world. Besides, you are a pure example of these fortuitous encounters ! The path is everywhere, its actors countless. You will learn wisdom and control of forces.

It is a work of self-moderation in the face of the exuberant forces of nature, a power that can only be soothed for a time, until the forces get back in motion and dominate us again. The middle way soothes briefly the now. The way of moderation against all extremes. A stanza that dives the philosopher into a strange meditative state for a brief moment.

Mikaël : The path is in me as it is in you. Some quote sentences and follow preconceived ideas, their quotations are correct, but not the meaning given to them. They are emptied of their spirit. I understood long ago that scholarship does not protect against certain occult forces, that there were actions of good and evil, that one does not exist without the other.

Doc Faust : Always live in the now, the past has passed, live in consciousness Nature, the World, the Divine... put order back into it. The main problem is the imbalance of forces and the choices that the penitent will make according to himself. Namely : choosing the luminous or dark side of the force. It's like a science fiction book, but reality often goes beyond fiction. We do not fight for good or against evil, but for the respect of a certain balance. Being in truth and harmony at all times, in the thought of the action, of the word that has not yet been spoken, of the right thought, is not easy every day. We must work on it, not to say muzzle our senseless ardour as fallen men, for we forget that we are only mere humans dressed in the appearance of our qualities, but mostly tainted by our defects.

There, I put you in the state of mind to continue the alchemical work : I make the void in you so you can be filled again, as we do with matter. It is released (empty) from the black light (released light) and then filled with the original light : it is a manifested light.

Gate of Notre Dame of Chartes, the tetramorph

Alchemical introduction through the middle way

The Grail is only the cup but has inside a light that shines outside. The Adepts say : "One body, one vessel, one fire". What they fail to say is that this truth is gazed *a posteriori* and is by no means a starting point for projecting oneself into the future. It is like realizing, after the act, that we have gone from *materia prima* to *prima materia*.

Mikaël : Like in that quote from Lao Tzu that comes to my mind :

*"Thirty spokes converge to the hub,
but the emptiness between them makes the tank move forward.
A clod of clay is used to make the jar,
but it is the emptiness within that gives it its use.
Walls, doors, and windows make the house,
but the emptiness of the room makes it possible to live there.
Matter is useful, immaterial gives true use.*

This reminds me of the work in the laboratory - which consists in distilling an alcohol - when the matter works in the balloon and becomes spiritual. Everything happens through fire control, there is sublimation in the retort neck, so that the spiritual appears as tears of blood emerging from the chest and water the little ones. Then, as it is said, it is necessary to cut off the head and tail of the dragon, i.e. throwing the mercurial sulphur at the beginning and the sulphurous mercury at the end.

Doc Faust : The key of a good heating is controlling the temperature. For this, you can use a sand bath, a cover bell, or even a variator that precisely harmonizes the heating up, there is no limit to your imagination. If I talk to you about all these elements, it's because the instruments are at the service of the operative as an extension of his thought. Too often, I have seen puffers thinking that it was their glassware that had a lack and that - in no way - the problem was a concern of harmony, a break between thought and instrument due to lack of reflection.

An experiment must be reproducible because, in fact, with the same actor, the same causes must produce the same effects. Under no circumstances should an experiment be pursued whose causes do not produce any of the expected effects, in the hope that they may be likely to change by a miracle. Some say that the actor has a place in the experience, yes, but only if the right assumptions are made and all the conditions are met.

Without truth, only lies live. If we see light appearing in matter, we shouldn't forget that from matter light or more precisely fire will spring back. It is simply a matter of time, a path that only needs to be opened up again. You were born dust and you will return dust, but shouldn't we say : "You were born light, you will meet darkness and you will return to the light" ?

Mikaël : At first, operating was tricky, but I found the right adjustment of the heating plate and the appropriated accessories, to maintain a precise temperature for a long time. The quality of the result depends on the temperature of the laboratory, the atmospheric pressure, the hygrometry... and thus the temperature can be controlled over time. After having adjusted by good practices, I will not fail to repeat the experience again and again by reflecting beforehand on the expected effects and not to wander aimlessly, slave of the reaction and the experience poorly conducted.

Doc Faust : Don't you think Ancient's were using thermometers ? They were using colors and yardsticks as markers, they were ingenious where scientific progress was still in its infancy. But in a more secular perspective, if you want to master the art of balloon fire, look at making a perfect egg. Madame's gourmet cuisine is often the backyard of a good alchemist.

One day I should resume our conversations with Hervé This[r], he knew how to transcend his training as a chemist to make the senses and tastes explode in molecular cuisine. I see in him a kind of alchemist on a path that crosses over with our art.

Mikaël : The fire trial –like when you challenged me to cook a perfect egg. I now see the analogy with alchemy and mastering of fire, both outside and inside.

Doc Faust : Obviously, who doesn't know how to perfectly cook an egg cannot become a good alchemist, he cannot understand and master the art of fire. The perfect egg is the first job from the oratory to the laboratory that the apprentice must master to enter the labyrinth.

This exercise easily measures how much someone is involved and the degree of trust it will implement in his relationship with the elements.

---

[r] Hervé This, born in 1955 is a french physical chemist. He's known to be the inventor – with Nicholas Kurti- of the molecular gastronomy, but also of the molecular cuisine.

Alchemical introduction through the middle way

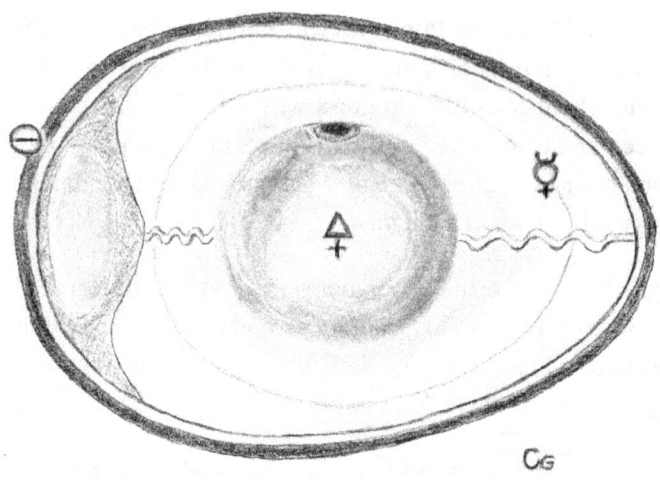

Mikaël : It is, indeed, a great initiation test and a real introduction to the subject that allows you to pass through a first door.

At the beginning we hold the 64°Celsius, we deposit the eggs sofltly and, whoops ! The temperature goes to 69°Celsius, so we change our strategy, we tinker, we try again and then we maintain precisely the 64°Celsius for 45 minutes, and it is won.

Usually, the egg is overcooked or undercooked, the perfect egg has a translucent white but neither liquid nor rubbery, the yolk is neither liquid nor plastery, when it is perfect... it is... unique.

Alchemical introduction through the middle way

The Salamander that feeds on the good fire.
Hôtel de Bourgtheroulde in Rouen

Doc Faust : It is a rather pleasant test to perform, and there is always an easy way to succeed without the use of technology but with just common sense. Alchemists make little use of the thermometer, they visualize temperatures in colours or standards. We practice according to the same principle in the crucible !

I call it the blind control method : you put a lead sheet in a second control crucible and when you see this lead melt, you know then that you have reached 327.5°C; and *de facto*, you know that the temperature is identical in your other crucible without looking at it. And it even works with another material. The Ancients didn't have an electronic probe like now. You don't use a jackhammer to break a nut

The Alchemical Laboratory

« *Our chimical operation are as follows : Sublimation, Dissolution, Filtration, Cohobation, Distillation, Separation, Reverberation, Impregnation and Digestion".* Aphorisms of Urbigerius

The laboratory is discretly hidden in the backyard garden, away from prying eyes. This place is very peaceful, there is a particular atmosphere, it is a place out of space and time.

Alchemical introduction through the middle way

Mikaël : Yesterday, at dawn, I delicately picked a few flowers from the lime tree, a remarkable tree that scents our garden and beyond. Freshly collected, I took them to the laboratory. I stop in the semi-darkness, a soft music harmoniously enveloping the alcove.

In the laboratory, I work for hours, grind, heat, separate and then assemble again. The extraction then takes shape, a wonderful emerald green color appears in the balloon. I will have to work for several days to collect the supreme elixir.

Until the quintessence is achieved, the waiting time between two operations is not lost, I dedicate it to meditation and reading. I am currently reading Basile Valentin's book[6] "The Twelve Keys to Philosophy" that I have just received.

Doc Faust : One day, I will come to bless your laboratory according to the rites of the elders, to put some of my magic into your home, it will be like connecting you to my universe. The links created that way are paths that will last forever. You can also read "Propos sur les deux Lumières" (*About the Two Lights*) by Henri La Croix Haute, which is easier to read than Henri Coton-Alvart's "*Les Deux Lumières*" (*The Two Lights*). Buddhists say "We cannot know everything, but we should start by appreciating what we already know".

Mikaël : *The two Lights...* Yes, this book is fundamental. It is my bedside book. It is quite difficult to read but so luminous in the same time. It needs to be "distil", it is hard to approach the conception of a light that has two natures : the original or uncreated light and the released light,...

Alchemical introduction through the middle way

Doc Faust : It is not that hard actually, without betraying a secret, I can summarize this conception by the vision of a world in two bubbles[7] juxtaposed (even if there is, in the end, an infinity of bubbles). Nature is a great watchmaker who only initiates its universal mechanism by pouring light flows from one bubble into another and then starting all over again. We are in the second bubble. A bubble that receives the light of the first bubble to create matter in the second one ("non-light" or by equivalent darkness surrounded by light). Seen from our bubble the light of the first bubble is invisible and increated, like Isis veiled from appearances (which by the way is veiled from the colors of the Work). Once done or created in the first buble, the light can be considered as an original light. When this light goes from the first to the second buble, then it is (original) light manifested.

What the philosopher will call the *philosopher stone* is only so pure and so aligned matter that it will be used as a vessel to the original light. This matter is a light trap that temporarily locks it in this state and, as a result, becomes a manifested light. This manifested light applies its magical power on the surrounding matter when it is released.

Mikaël : This is an interesting approach, understanding the es-sence (the sense) of the world ! It don't strive after mastering it all, or having an opinion on everything, but at least to understand what I know and to feel where is the essential. To capture the essence of heaven as a "divine" word, or words of truth.

Some of the traditional alchemists advise me to approach astrology, the tarot, to work in the laboratory according to the phases of the sun and the moon, to work with plants according to the theory of signatures, to practice the day when the color of the flower is in association with the color of one of the seven planets[s], at a particular time, and that one cannot progress in alchemy without all this. Do we really have to submit to all this knowledge and practices to approach the Great Art ?

Doc Faust : Astrology, Tarot, ... All of this is fascinating, but why scatter ? Many confuse allegory and literal meaning of the texts. Alchemy is the basis of everything and not the other way around, so please, let's keep it simple in here ! We should stop diluting ourselves by seeking to know on all subjects... Each one has his own way, but an alchemist is only an astrologer to live his daily life. For the spagyrus, the sun and the moon are the only two stars that have a strong influence on our earth, they symbolize the duality of sulphur and mercury. Herbal medicine was called "*simplicis medicinae*"(medicine of the simple). So let's stay in that spirit !

Mikaël : Those who don't understand read even more, and therefore progress even slower. Moreover, they have to invent new concepts to get lost deeper in the maze... Anyway each one has his own way ! However, extracting plants is fun, and allows you to get familiar with the instruments in the laboratory. I even make some modifications to the equipment. All this work is useful to the future alchemist, and it opens many doors !

Doc Faust : *You're beginnig to free yourself from the instrument, that's good ! You adapt it to your own* experiences ! You use the

---

[s] See « board of planets » on the appendix (p. 317)

reflections on the plant pathway to transpose it to the other pathways : mineral and animal. Remember, Alchemy began for you from the moment you inspired and then exhaled... This is the cycle of Ouroboros[t], whether it was with an apterous snake or assisted by a second wing.

Mikaël : Always keep it simple, that is so comforting ! It is said "What is above is like what is below", so when we talk about astrology in alchemy, it is an allegory that must be attached to what is below.

Doc Faust : Ebb and Flow, the one who becomes aware that he is breathing performs his first work as an alchemist. I'm telling you : the more I learn, the more I know that I don't know anything. For like any word of truth, it will move you forward and by your progress you will strengthen those words to go even further. The limit of our understanding is moving back much faster than the strength of our progress, it seems unoptimistic and yet that is what success is all about, increasing the choice of possibilities faster than we can explore their possibilities. The trap is the stagnation by the lack of new fields of exploration

---

[t] "Ouroboros : the snake eating is own tail, is the symbol of an evolution circle but withdrawn on itself. This symbol his about ideas of movement, continuity, self-fertilization, eternal return. The circular shape of the image proposes the union of the terrestrial world (chthonian), represented by the snake, and the celestial world represented by the circle."
Dictionary of the symbols J. Chevalier and A. Gheerbrant. *(TN : Translated from the french).*

The three alchemical roses

Mikaël : When we say : Inhale/exhale, Ebb/Flow, Action/Reaction, the alchemicals baselines are then very well established, isn't it ?

Doc Faust : With one you make two, but mostly with two you make one. That's how you read a Tetractys.

When you get that you can see the treasure (*trésor,* as the three *(trois, tres)* pink golden *(ors)* at Brussels or Cluny*)*. Aren't the black, the white and the Crimson, the three golden (*"trois-or"*) ? Going through the three colors of the Work, the three kingdoms of nature, the body, the soul, the spirit, the sulfur, the mercury and the salt ! This is why the three flowers don't look the same in the vessel, because they are seen at three different stages of the work.

On the same idea, we can see that the magical numbers are : Three – the Apprentice ; Five – The companion ; Seven : the master or accomplished man, and Ten – God, as in the sephirotic tree
.

The Tetractys[u]

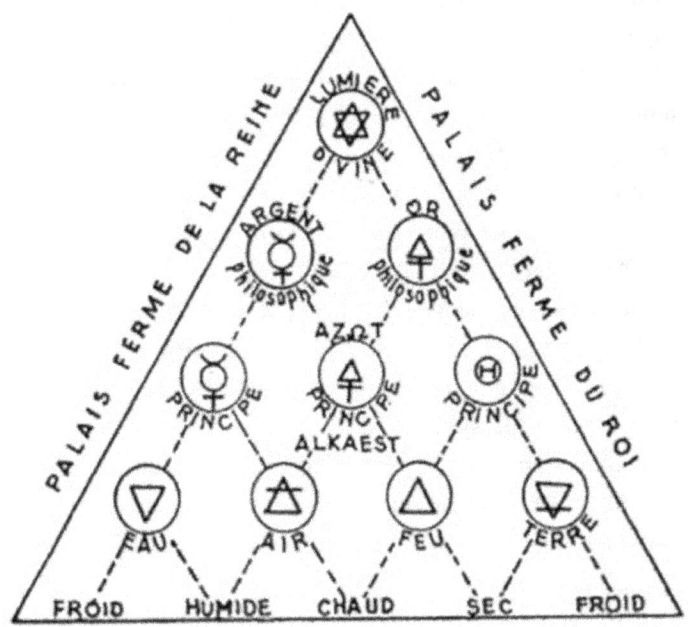

"The Tetractys in which is found the source and the root of eternal nature. Evertyhing comes from the decade and goes back to it. The 10 is the image of the wholeness in motion."

---

[u] Palais fermé de la reine = Closed palace to the queen / Palais fermé du roi = Closed palace to the king / Lumière divine = Divine light / Argent philosophique = Philosophical silver / Or philosophique = Philosophical gold / Eau = Water / Air = Air / Feu = Fire / Terre = Earth / Froid = Cold / Humide = Wet / Chaud = Hot / Sec = Dry

Mikaël : Pythagoras' Tetractys[8] ! The reason why it is said that everything is easy and hard in the same time. I worked hard on its components, because - from the beginning- I felt it was essential to understand its elements and analogies... I collected some old representations in order to progress in its understanding. Thus, in order to let it sink in as best as I could, I completed it with a few notes according to my current beliefs and then formalized it with a sketch. But this is the work that everyone should do to in order to improve themselves ! And come back to it as much as they need it. In the end, this triangle is alive because it is reconstructed by the time and the geometer's understanding. The entire realization of the alchemical work is contained and explained by the Tetractys[V]. We just need to look at synonyms, to associate everything we know about the alchemical bestiary or allegories found in the texts of the ancients. Then we must put our minds at the service of our hearts and the doors open by themselves one after the other. That's the key !

Doc Faust : One who know how to ear will find his path by himself in the shades of knowledge. Moreover to show you how important it

---

[V] "We see in this graphic above (which was confirmed to be perfectly accurate by J. Boucher, who had received a similar one from his master Fulcanelli), that Cold and Humid generate Water, Humid and Hot generate Air, Hot and Dry generate Fire, and Dry and Cold generate Earth. Then, Water and Air generate Mercury Principle, Air and Fire generate Sulfur Principle, and Fire and Earth generate Salt Principle. In the second stage of the work, Mercury Principle and Sulfur Principle generate Philosophical Silver or Silver of the Wise, and Sulfur Principle and Salt Principle generate Philosophical Gold or Gold of the Wise. The coupling of the two then gives the Chrysopoeia". Text and drawing from "L'alchimie spirituelle"(*Spiritual Alchemy*) by R. Ambelain.

Alchemical introduction through the middle way

is to beware of what seems to be granted, I will show you my Tetractys (relatively close to Henri Coton-Alvart's) and not Jules Boucher's which he claims to have been confirmed by Fulcanelli.

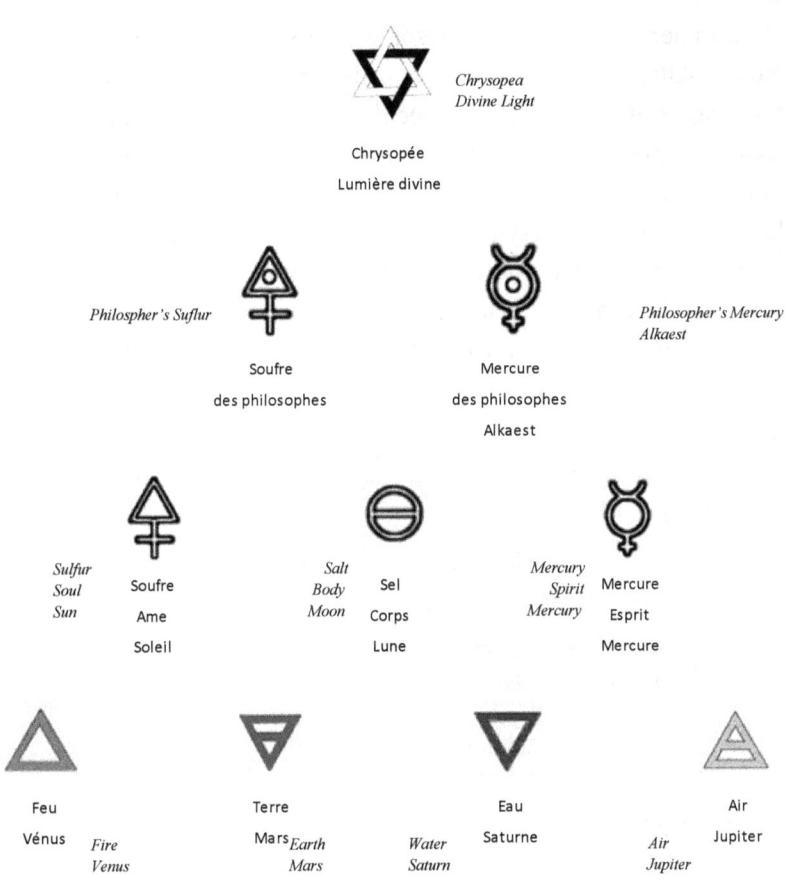

We might notice in this Tetractys, adapted to the Alchemist's way of understanding rythms, that the sun and the moon are down back to the rank of the three principles instead of the philosopher's sulfur and mercury. The idea is to respect the reference to the 4+3=7 planets, basis of our triangulation. If we would we could take, as some text are suggesting, the philosopher's sulfur as the philosopher's sun and the philosopher's mercury as the philosopher's moon. Alternative choices are possible and most welcome. As Raymond Lulle in his "Chrysopée du Seigneur"(*Lord's Chrysopoeia*) some people think that the Wisdom rank his higher than the Philosophy one. Others put Philosophy and Wisdom on the same level. We must always consider the context and accept some divergences because, the autor's logic matters most than the exact shape of the triangle. Truths are evolving because alchemical truths are constantly changing. *Nothing is constant except change.*

Apocalypse 1 :8

Ego sum Alpha et Omega, principium et finis, dicit Dominus Deus, qui est et qui erat et qui venturus est Omnipotens.

Εγώ ειμι το Αλφα και το Ωμεγα, λέγει κύριος ο θεός, ο ων και ο ην και ο ερχόμενος, ο παντοκράτωρ.

I'm the Alpha and Omega, beginning and end, said the Lord, Who is, was and is to come, the Almighty. *

* *translated from the Latin version.*

Alchemical introduction through the middle way

*Introduction of the child Jesus to the three Wise men.
Engraving - Monastery of San Martin in Santiago de Compostela*

Mikaël : What are, according to you, the effects of the light on our thoughts, on our bodies ?

Doc Faust : The image that comes to my mind is the cross with a rose on its center. Your question also make me think about some various words : Causality, Synchronity, Amplification, Propagation, Deflagration, Return Shock !

This is what you feel when you absorb light or, more precisely, when light crosses you whith its rays. You will not come out unscathed : you are the Whole... and the universe is part of you. So if the universe controls you in its infinity, you, a small receiver of light at the level of a particle, you will find yourself with the power to influence this infinity.

It is a bit like the example of the mathematician who would talk to his student about the manifestation of unusual phenomena using the law of chaos as a model.

He would explain that it consists in watching a butterfly flap its wings in Asia and contemplating its effects as a hurricane in the United States[w]. The cause and effects are often inversely proportional when you are alone with nature.

---

[w] The "butterfly effect" is a metaphor for the fundamental phenomenon of sensitivity to the initial conditions of chaos theory. The exact wording that gave rise to it was expressed by Edward Lorenz at a scientific conference in 1972, by the following question: "Can the flapping of a butterfly's wings in Brazil cause a tornado in Texas ?

We are interconnected

Highlight of the contact between two corpuscles. Even if they are distanced from each other they continue to be connected by a manifested wave.

"The concept of interdependence goes to the core of reality and its implications are tremendous. Can phenomena exist by themselves ? Or to what extent are they interconnected ? The EPR phenomenon and the Foucault pendulum experiment suggest that wholeness is the very essence of reality.*"

Trinh Xuan Thuan

*TN : Translated from the French

Mikaël : I have always been convinced, and even more, I have always *felt* that everything was intimately linked, atom to atom. No matter how much you bomb the atoms with energy and light, you can only interfere with their shape. The smallest particle and the most distant in the universe are intimately linked to our being, everything vibrates in unison (unique sound). Nature follows that logic and vibrates in sound and light, well, according to our human conception. When we understand this, we are in tune with the great Whole. But there is still a lot of work to be done. On this topic, I have read and encourage you to do the same the admirable book "Le Cosmos et le Lotus"(*the cosmos and the Lotus*) by astrophysicist Trinh Xuan Thuan[x].

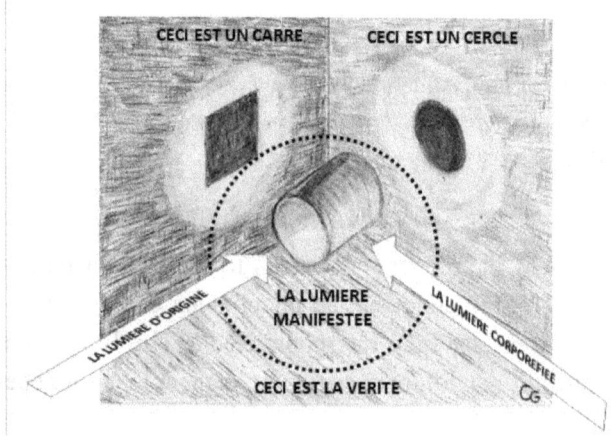

It's all about perspective (From a drawing of the "Copenhagen school")

---

[x] Trinh Xuan Thuan, born in 1948 in Hanoï, Vietnam, is a Vietnamese-American writer and astrophysicist, who mostly writes in French.

Alchemical introduction through the middle way

Doc Faust : Vibrating a Tibetan bowl is an interesting experience for an Alchemist. It allows you to understand the relationship between the apprentice and his material. You make it ring and the bowl rings back, you give some of your light, and you receive some original light, you add water in your bowl and the water becomes a filter to the waveform. The truth is always there, but different as if there were several alternative truths according to where you are.

The wave trans-*forms* itself, until the perfect convergence that we can also find in transparency. The exchange of information does not require contact, ebb and flow occurs regardless of the distance between two people, provided they are aligned.

Mikaël : As when you randomly arrange various tuning forks of different frequencies, but some of them have the same note. If you hit one of the twins, the second will resonate with it.

Doc Faust : I'm as this tuning fork, a light transmitter. If you just listen, without syncronizing on the same frequency you don't change yourself ; that is why we talk about *Âme-Our (*Amour = Love ; *Âme =Soul*). This state of being allows you to free yourself from you own life, in order to be able to fill up with others light. In the Egyptian mythology *BA* is the depiction of the divine inspiration on earth, and *OUR*, described as the sun's eyes, characterizes the heavens. We find a similar symbolism with the Greek's Alpha and Omega.

If you put an atom in front of another one, and the put them very far away from each other, they will always be in communication. It is one of the phenomenon that the quantum physicians are studying.

Mikaël : But, what we ususally call waves and vibrations... isn't it a simplistic interpretation to name what makes all things move ? Plato in his time and others before him were already asking themselves this question.

About waves, vibrations and the connexion between the livings and the universe : Pernelle and I are giving, since a few years, holistic and energetic treatments, according to an ancient knowledge from Tibet. We are adapting this ancient practice of energy passage and chakra balancing according to our feelings and experience on people with pain and suffering, and this gives convincing results

This practice matches perfectly to a thinking of universal and positive connectivity. We have been, as in the spirit of alchemy, graciously educated and we are the thirteenth generation in the lineage of Mikao Usui. This Buddhist monk was taught during a retreat on Mount Kurama-Yama and has been spreading Reiki since the beginning of the 20th century. In the same spirit, we provide this care on a voluntary basis to people in need, nevertheless sometimes people insist on giving us some money, which we systematically give back to people in need. Being instituted at the highest level of discipline, we will teach this knowledge, for free, to others.

Doc Faust : Mikaël, you know probably much more than I do about vibrations and the vital energy. In fact, energy and light are two different words used to cure the same physiological disorders, so it works approximately the same. Remember that what you don't discover by yourself will only lead you to dead ends. You are right to adapt energy care, to make the connection between what you want and what you know. The only thing I ask you to do is being gratefull when you use someone else's technique, and never forget to mention his name.

Now, about all these trends, which I -probably wrongly- call "*New Age*", we must remain very rational when we broach onto phenomena that science cannot explain, otherwise we run the risk to get lost. We must make these esoterics experiments compatible with scientific rigour.

Mikaël : We can use some ideas and traditions of the buddhists monk in our everyday life : chakra, chanting bowls, mantras, plants, water, ... We can try everything, but wisely. This is very close of the spirit of the energetic healings treatments.

Doc Faust : Be carefull, I often saw that the energetics healers were focusing on the shape of the symbols. Don't forget that the Ki^y is active, and even "intelligent" and indépendand. It is as en entity that develops itself and support the treatment. Actually, you could be doing the same thing with any music instrument. The Alchemy is a music score played by the musician. You just need to be on the right path with "only the intention to". We find again what we said earlier, we transpose the "practitionner – treatment – sick people" into "alchemist – instrument - matter".

Mikaël : It's a fact, the initiation teaches us some rituals and opening symbols, but the purpose is to channel the energy, in all its shapes. Rituals and symbols, used by the novice, are only ways of firmly fixing things between oneself ant the Universe. They help us to connect faster. Those archetypes[9] are part of ourselves, as Jung

---

[y] Ki : Japanese name expressing the notion of universal energy.

perfectly said in "Psychology and Alchemy". Everyone has to adapt others' rituals with their own feeling, it can help to refocus.

Doc Faust : Jung didn't understood much about alchemy, but as a self-taught explorer, he had the merit of intuitively formalizing the part beyond alchemy, the part you acquire when you become a philosopher through fire.

Intuition without global understanding is only a fragmented vision of the subject : no cause, no purpose, no effect. However, the book shouldn't be rejected, it just needs to be shifted in the right place and as always, to be read with discernment while keeping his own free will as an alchemist.

Under no circumstances should you go into the madness of the psychiatrist who is much sicker than his own patients !

Indeed, energetic healing techniques come from a specialization of the alchemy medicine. It is like an alchemy based on good thought that you pass to others. Its transfering mode depends on your original culture, as a shaman would do with its tutelary animals. It is the purity of the message that matters. As for the man, because he is made like this, he can swing between good and bad.

Mikaël : Unfortunately in the practicing of the energetics care, we encouter the same issues than in alchemy or other fields : people seeking for power, recognition, etc. are darkening our purification work. Those various practices of tibetan care are often plagiarized, people trying to hide their true origin, in order to make some money of it, and its very harmful.

Alchemical introduction through the middle way

Doc Faust : Remember that those who don't know talk to much and say many wrong things. It's a helpful way to see the tendencies they have to the force.

Proceeding as they do, without thinking, is like trying to understand philosophy by studying the definitions in the dictionary.

Mikaël : The important thing is to have a new water, and let the dirty water go out.

A surveyor on the path

The Adept on the cathedral of Santiago the Compostela

In the ancient Egypt, the surveyor used the knotted rope to draw the plans of the temples. They were built using this tool called "Toth's Line". Toth being the sacred ibis whose step length determined the divine cubits. So the measurements of the temple are the measurements of Toth, the one who establishes the ordinance, the expert, the exact and the just.

Alchemical introduction through the middle way

Mikaël : But Doc, by dints of walking the paths, who are you ?

Doc Faust : I am very little in the end, by dint of cutting my stone, I just become a witness of our time, a light giver. My duty is to share and spread the alchemical philosophy and, from time to time, to help in the laboratory. I remember the conclusion of Paulo Coelho's book "The Alchemist"[z], which, like the ouroboros, speaks of a distant treasure, of a long road that the penitent must travel, while it is right at our feet. Some would say, "If I knew, I wouldn't have made such a long trip." They forget that the treasure is not at the end of the road, but all along it. I searched for a long time for masters, in fact, I only came across *centimeters*. And from time to time, real initiates, who were unfortunately calamitous teachers. So I moved away and came back to find wisdom at my origins, that is, within myself. The Adept who had lived in me for so long then appeared, as the "*Fiat Lux*" of creation, and with this truth, the Truth ... because in the beginning was the Word... of alchemical philosophy.

Mikaël : Isn't it an end in itself to be happy to serve ? I was helped from an early age, in the scientific field, by beautiful people. If the heart is open, you are immediately immensely rich.

When I was fifteen, I spend a month on a holiday by the sea. I met Bernard, who was old as my father, yet led me into beautiful philosophical discussions : life, science, the creation of the universe,... The discussions with him lasted several years. He was only a humble philosopher and yet he shared his knowledge

---

[z] "O Alquimista » printed by Planeta in 1988, and in English in 1993 by HarperTorch.

generously. This unexpected encounter, these intense and memorable moments will remain forever treasured in my heart.

Doc Faust *:* Often, I heard that the naughty little chemist could never succeed, and yet... I prefer the scientist who will be able to make the smart connection between established science and the great Art, than those with preconcieved ideas.

Some sparks can turn into fires with a little help. It took me four decades to get to where I am today. Years of uninterrupted work, often lonely, sometimes accompanied. I lived moments of doubt, but each time, a sign showed me the way and strengthened my faith.

It is easier now to talk and reserch about Alchemy. In the 80's they was no internet, only really expansive books. Fortunately, knowledge does not stop with the lack of technology and knows how to find its way to come and meet us. So I had the light almost ten years ago. I was then close to my forty's.

This divine spark that is in ourselves is widely evoked in Indian mythology !

"An old Hindu legend tells that once upon a time all men were Gods but they abused their divine state so much that Brahma -the Master of Gods- decided to take away their divine power and hide it in a place where it would be impossible to find. The bigest problem was then to find this hiding place.

Alchemical introduction through the middle way

When the minor Gods were summoned to a council to solve this problem, they suggested the following : Bury the human's divine essence in the Earth.

But Brahma said : No, it isn't enough, because Men will dig it and find it. So, the Gods said : In this case, throw this divine essence in the depths of the oceans. But again, Brahma said : "No, because, sooner or later, Men will explore the depths of all the oceans, and one day, will find it and will rise it to the surface. So minor Gods concluded : We don't know where to hide it because it seems that there isn't any place on earth or in the sea that Man won't be able to reach.

So, Brahma said : "Here is what we will do of Humans divine essence, we will hide it in the depths of his heart, for it is the only place where he will never think to seek it". Since then, man has been around the world, exploring, climbing, diving and digging, in search of something that is already inside him. "

Mikaël : It's a wonderful story. Men don't believe in themselves. If they knew that their divine essence is in their heart, they probably wouldn't make so many mistakes. Are men destined to destroy everything ? Look around us ! In the Bible it is written : after the Fall, God send us Jesus to save humanity. But apparently He hasn't achieved His work yet.

Doc Faust : All the prophets are in fact only anomalies of history that seek to manipulate the mind of the modern man. It is like the magician who, with his card tricks or dexterity, uses illusion to make you believe he is a messiah. The truth is that magic does not exist in the hands of another, only you create it.
But Mikaël, what are you actually looking for ?

Mikaël : For a long time, I have been searching for the truth about the world, the universe, eternity, the very notion of God, to change objects and mentalities. In other words to elevate myself as much as possible and to help those seeking for wisdom and who would like to go back to the original Word. You often talk to me about the Holy Spirit, can you tell me more about it ? My friends regularly ask me about religion : Should an alchemist be by nature a believer, a practitioner ? The Old Testament is clearly symbolic, but what about the New Testament ? Should it be understood as a historical truth or rather as symbols and a series of myths mixed with very real facts (in particular the life of Jesus, his crucifixion, his resurrection) ? Haven't we made an amalgam between the story of a committed man – probably initiated - and a "Life Force" that we still don't know how to give any explanation ? And hasn't all this been taken up by men looking for power ?

Alchemical introduction through the middle way

Doc Faust : Picture this, men discovering an universal science, but they are only a few, surrounde d by a chaotic mankind. The others are busy killing each others in order to possess some wealth. They will need to manipulate myhts and legends, to forge stories of Gods and saviors… This kind of storytelling always have a great impact on the minds, and thanks to the fear they inspire, they stay forever in our memories.

If, you built a religion around superstions, if you save Men from their crimes, if you build churches that will stay for centuries… You could then, between all those nonsenses, put some wise words of true philosophers.

Thus was born the allegory and *language of birds*[10], the profane sense and the hidden sense, stone books in churches as the art of practicing mass and hymns. Religions, on their profane sides were called upon to force man to find more peace, but the hidden language made it possible to perpetuate the true knowledge of the creator and His benefits.

God doesn't exist ! He never did ! But that doesn't mean that there is nothing, that there isn't a creator. God only forgot to invent himself a human shape. Mankind is only an epiphenomenon, an irregularity destined to disappear over time. This is why light strives to try -in vain- to dissolve us and to make us join our creator once our earthly existence has ended.

Alchemical introduction through the middle way

But, let's consider that there is actually a God that created us, and with the story of Brahma, Shiva et Vishnu[aa] let's see how the most ancient religion reaches our most advanced science.

At first, in the Universe, we have the original movement which is the condition to the existence of space and time. This original movement, called the "*fiat lux*", is a ray of light that can take three kinds of forms to propagate : circular, rectilinear or helical. Any released light that circulates and makes an encounter alters the shape of the object still called darkness. Darkness being impenetrable non-light, light will come to wrap itself around this non-light nucleus and form what is called matter surrounded by energy or corpuscles.

Brahma	Shiva	Vishnou
Intelligence in motion	Willingness	Love and wisdom
⟳	⬇	〰
Circular movement that uses tiume	Straight movement that uses space	Helical movement that uses time ans space

---

[aa] Brahma: God creator of the world in its multiplicity, Shiva: God destroyer of the old man, of his attachments, of his beliefs, of his individual self. He destroys the old to move on to renewal. Vishnu: protective and conservative god of the world, in charge of watching over its evolution, without ever destroying it, he naturally descends into the world whenever his intervention appears necessary.

We don't know what light is, but we do know its radiation effects on matter. When the original light manifests itself, it will wrap itself around darkness, create matter that over time will be released again and make the matter disappear by leaving the darkness or dark matter again.

Light and Philosopher's stone

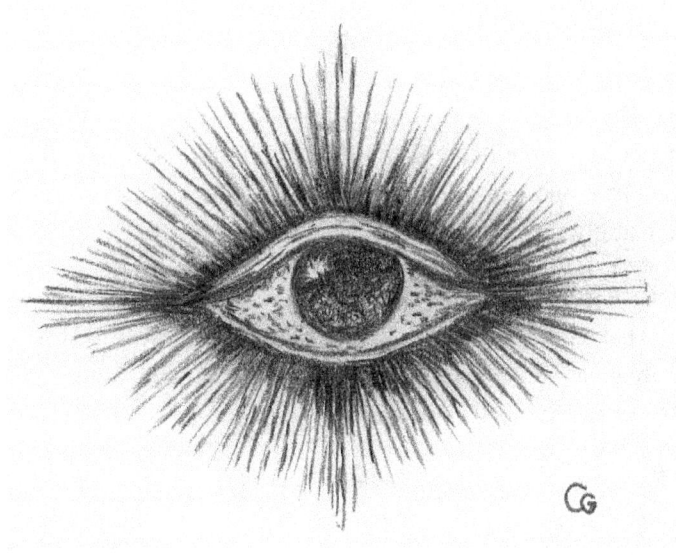

" In the beginning was the Word ...

... And the Word was with God, and the Word was God. Through him all things were made; without him nothing was made that has been made. In him was life, and that life was the light of all mankind. The light shines in the darkness, and the darkness has not overcome it."*

St John's Gospel 1 :1-5

* NIV ©1973, 1978, 1984, 2011 by Biblica, Inc.®

Alchemical introduction through the middle way

Doc Faust : The light manifested can appear in a mineral but also in a human body. The philosopher's stone is immaterial, the Grail (because in the divine we have the Father, the "Christ" and the Holy Spirit) is only a support of manifestation where it is temporarily fixed.

This is why no one can own the philosopher's stone, but only observe its effects for a time in a crystal that is only the receptacle, the sacred chalice. This one can itself, without being light, possess some of its states, namely : its color, its texture, its strength.

Mikaël : For the one who would have "obtained" the philosopher's stone, what is the path from chaos to enlightenment ? How do we know that we have obtained the philosophers' chrysopheus ? Are there several ways ? Several matters ?

Doc Faust : The philosopher's stone is a light attracted into a material whose crystalline mesh has been restructured after a long process of purification, rectification and alignment of its weft. With the accumulation of this work, some have even talked about magnetization, the material passes from the most absolute opaque to the most crystalline transparent, as would a piece of coal that would turn into a diamond. The accumulation of light will produce a red to pigeon blood red at its end.

But as a chemist friend told me, in nature you can produce any of the colours of the alchemical work with your experiments because the chromatic range is only the result of lighting, absorption and reflection. Henri Coton-Alvart goes even further by talking about different diameters of ray light, I wouldn't go that far.

Our Lord's chrysopoeia obtained, it isn't even necessary to prove it by transmutation, it is only the puffers who proceed to this kind of exhibition. The day you have the light manifested, you are no longer the same neither internally nor externally. You have to live it to understand it !

Mikaël : There are many qualities attributed to the philosophers' stone. So many that it seems impossible. Some say it would be able to create medicines from the three kingdoms, to reconstitute corrupted DNA, to grow crystalline gems in precious stones, to repeat the liquid stone in the luminescent stage.

Rumors even say that today art has really progressed : it would allow to modify the structure of steel and glass by making them transparent or opaque to light, it would allow to stop the nuclear fusion of a nucleus, to connect to the universal knowledge heritage of humanity, to move our thoughts in space and time...

Doc Faust : Well, I wish you to approach this truth and much more... As the eternal lamp observed by Carter in Egypt during his archaeological excavations (it is a luminous liquid of purple color that radiates alone) you will find in churches red coloured photophores, by analogy, but the purple liquid light is not red phosphorus as I may have heard !

Mikaël : Wasn't phosphorus discovered by the German alchemist Brant, and then a few years later by the English Boyle ? They were working on their urine thinking that it was the possible raw material and, by serendipity, discovered phosphorus.

Doc Faust : True, but the eternal lamp isn't phosphorus, and is very often in the oratories of the initiates. This witness is a reiteration of the philosopher's stone placed in a light bulb. It is the light manifested at the ultimate stage before its disappearance from the material world and its return to the origin.

Mikaël : So when, in a cathedral, at noon, the sunlight passes through a stained glass window, or, as in a crystal at Notre Dame de Bayeux where it illuminates the paving on the ground : Is it the light manifested ? As in the photo of the octagon crossed by a vertical and a horizontal bar, as if forming a cross ?

Doc Faust : This phenomenon is just an illustration of the alignment with the projected line of light. But we are here in the secular domain, so everyone is free to name it as they want. In any case, luminous artifacts are attracted to the spirit becoming "holy" and once the correction is made, the light - that will then be called the Holy Spirit - will gather the Body and the Soul.

In the same spirit, in Chartres Cathedral, at the time of the summer solstice at precisely noon solar time, a line of light passing through a stained glass window drilled for this purpose is projected onto the paving exactly at the point of the attachment of a small round crest set with a certain philosophical star. As only the attachment remains, it is customary to speak of the nail of St. John's Day in reference to the summer solstice. For us philosophers, it is the revelation of a certain operation in the work.

Mikaël : So, if I get it right, the Bayeux crystal crossed at noon, itself made up of the three principles, is waiting to receive the light ?

Alchemical introduction through the middle way

The alignment – Stained-glass window of the cathedral Notre Dame de Bayeux.

Here, the junction momentarily realized between Light and crystal, binds the Corpus to the Animus and offers this effect to the eye of the layman.

Doc Faust : It depicts the process of illumination of the philosopher's stone... In the projection of the ray of light, we also see duality since the shadow-matter persists as an obstacle to light. To do this, the crystal must be pure and aligned so that the light gushes inside (the full is the void) but above all it should be trapped without any possibility to leave.

It's similar to the relationship between man and matter. Man-matter alignment and synchronization allows matter to receive light and then, through reciprocity, to radiate on the man who is illuminated by it.

And as : "Which is above is like unto that which is below", once man is enlightened, he becomes bound to the universe. This is the miracle

Alchemical introduction through the middle way

of only one thing : In one the Whole ! The reunification of the top and the bottom by a spiritual bond, the Hermes messenger between gods and men.

Likewise, white does not exist without black, darkness is manifested by the illumination.

So there are black holes, white holes and, when everything is aligned, light holes ! The white holes are like gushing fountains, the black ones are vacuum cleaners of light and energy. The light holes are at the border between everything and nothing, it is a balance between light and matter, they are spirals of light surrounding the non-matter.

This is what Philosopher's glass does, it attracts, captures, retains but does not fix the light; transmutation is a release of this light that not fixed can be set free. The message of a perfect new form within the altered metallic meshes that only want to transform themselves back into what they were at the origin.

This is why gold is unalterable over time and cannot oxidize, the crystalline mesh is perfectly rectified, aligned, unalterable... well almost. The projection of the wave on an imperfect mesh rectifies it (rolls it up and unwinds it after rectification). This is how we move from light to matter and from matter to light.

You know that one can become enlightened simply by prayer. You could very well obtain enlightenment by practicing energetic healing. It is a question of harmony between you and the universe, a moment of stillness where you communicate and where an exchange is made, you ask and you receive. But let's say that mineral alchemy is the

Alchemical introduction through the middle way

path most travelled by Westerners, they need to touch, to see to believe... such as St Thomas.

The royal way, or middle way, goes crescendo and fixes the stages (the path) between the pilgrim and his material through adventures and encounters (archetypes). Each meeting is a test (door) that the penitent must pass successfully (keys) to progress.

Mikaël : Yes, I guess so, we are materialists, we need concrete things to be able to let go. It is "easier" with a medium in the laboratory, the operation in the furnace is a help, so that the exchange of Man-Matter is facilitated.

Doc Faust : The exchange of matter-human-matter sets a universal moment in an *"every moment"* temporality. The secret is to understand that light is intelligent and incorporeal. It is a wave that coexists with corpuscles. It connects souls together, more precisely, it acts as a messenger. Light is the consecrated link : Corpus - Animus - Spiritus.

This is what you find with the seven chakras and the animation of the seven rays as performers of energy care. As matter is an obstacle to light, disease is also an obstacle to light that must be overcome and driven out.

But what we don't say is that matter is dark and surrounded by light captured on the periphery. We can call it the fixation of light by darkness. Light whose speed has curved; what some people perceive without light as dark matter as they lack of grey matter.

Light is to a tear of the creator what matter is to darkness, and indeed associated with the devil[bb]. The matter will never cease to disintegrate as it is repeated with the original light - as a worn away of time- but it will never disappear, it just changes shape.

Mikaël : Matter is therefore the result of consciousness, because in fact, following the symbolic Fall expressed in the Bible, man brings awarness in matter, "God" in the Light.

Doc Faust : God made man fall, or rather man fell alone, God having not been fast enough to hold him back. Then God, in his infinite goodness, sends Christ the Redeemer so that the man-matter may be recomposed through the original message delivered, to the light.

Mikaël : Man misunderstands the message, he sees dogma and dogma blinds him.

We should rather understand the alchemical meaning of the Trinity in this way : Christ-Corpus-Salt-Space / God the Father-Animus-Sulphur-Time / the Holy Spirit-Spiritus-Mercury-Movement. The lattest one being the "messenger" link between the other two.

Doc Faust : To explain the revelation, we will consider the two lights of the alchemists...

[bb] Devil : from the Greek diábolos, and diabállô, "diabolic" from the Greek dia-ballein: to disperse. Is has the same construction than "symbolic" or in Greek "syn-ballein" = to put together.

… a light from above

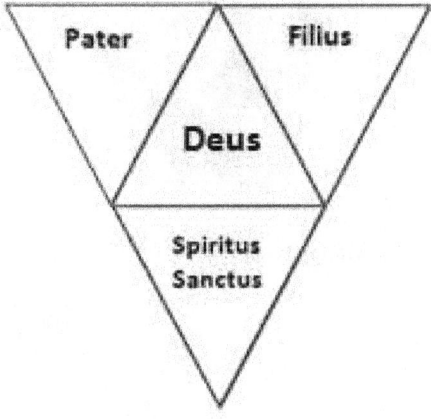

… a light from below

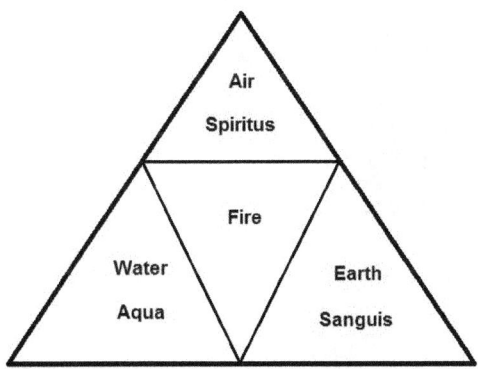

We will use these two lights to transform our coal (black opaque material) into diamonds. The two lights will help us in this transformation by manifesting the original light.

Alchemical introduction through the middle way

We will chase the darkness away by bringing it to light

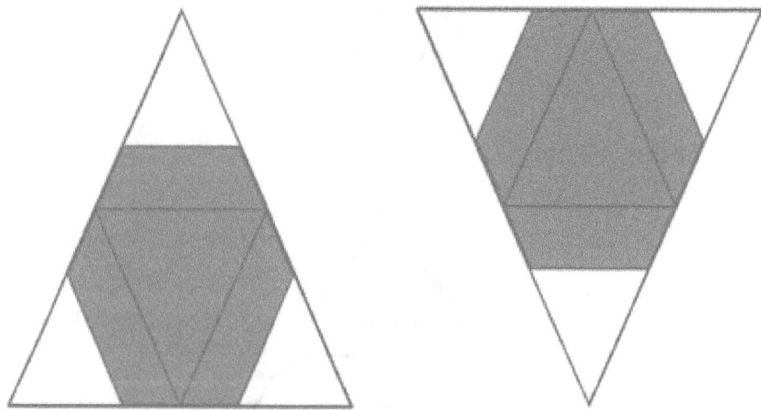

Light from below entering in the matter.

Light from above entering the matter.

When the fire from above meets the fire from below, or when the microcosm meets the macrocosm we obtain the chrysopoeia (from the Greek khrusōn : gold, and poiēin : to make) rectified and motionless in its center, where God is.

Alchemical introduction through the middle way

The alchemist sees in it the sanctuarization of yellow light and blue light to form a vertical reunification, where for an instant what is below is like what is above.

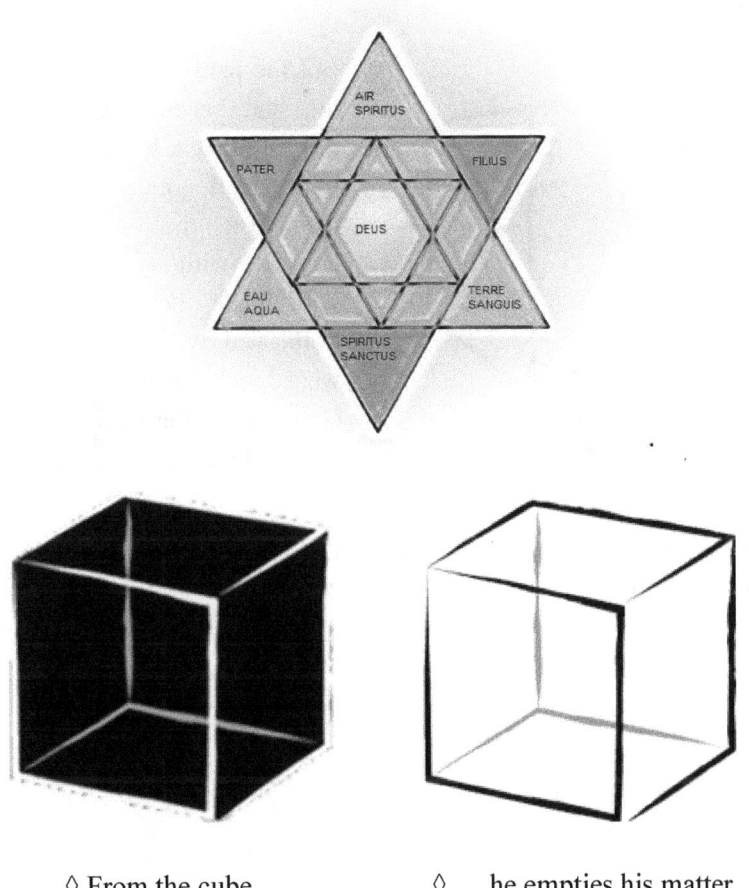

◊ From the cube... ◊ ... he empties his matter

Bringing together the Fire from above with the Fire from below is the goal of the alchemist's apprentice. To succeed in this work is to succeed in the purification process, which is materialized through transparency and stillness. The moment of the junction between the two lights allows the original light to pass through the matter and be temporarily manifested. For it is said that what is will return to what was.

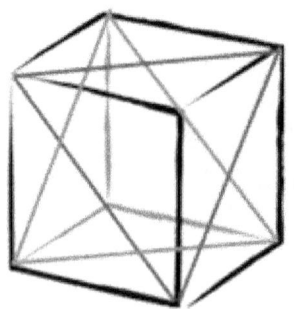

But the path is important up to the star, because according to the path taken, humility or ego, trade, gift, mercantilism or disinterest, the adept will be crowned with white or stained with black. For it is said in truth, you will not trade with what has been given to you by God, for otherwise you will have to face the Judgment.

Mikaël : This is very similar to the final phase of the Tetraktys. The mass is said :

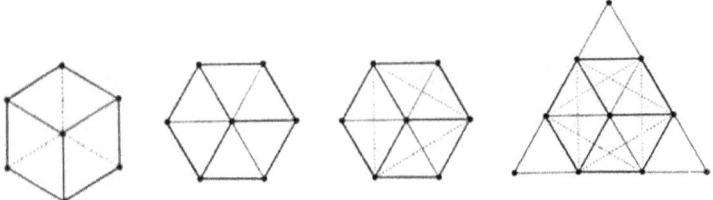

The Stone – The two lights – The tetraktys

Alchemical introduction through the middle way

Doc Faust : A glass hole between space and time, a stasis between light and matter.

Mikaël : Is it what we call Multiverses^z ?

Doc Faust : A multitude of universes, directions... Or perhaps a moment of union between the physical and the spiritual, holes like in the rat ball, passages letting the light enter from behind the veil of appearances. A journey downstream of the spirit and upstream in time, which allows predictions and prophecies, none of this is said in the books.

Mikaël : The same may be true for apparitions and other unexplained phenomena..... But we are going beyond the subject. You talk about light, matter, but how does the information of the World flow ?

Doc Faust : For the wide (or wise) steps to be taken, the apprentice will consider the matter as a void, the full is emptiness and the empty is the full, as David Bohm rediscovered it.

This new structure allows the circulation of information between the interstices of the net (one can even wonder if the mesh thread is not used as a vector for the orientation of the circulation of information and energy flows).

As for matter, it is only a temporal and formal organization that has the vocation to reorganize itself (I should say re-inform itself) and then to disappear with time in its halo of light. I find the expression that characterizes matter pretty : it is energy in condensed light

Alchemical introduction through the middle way

Statue of Isis veiled - Hoover Park - West Branch, Iowa In the United States.
"I am what has been, what is and what will be,
and no mortal has yet lifted the veil that covers me"

Mikaël : As in quantum physics ?

Mikaël : Yes, it is the physics of the smallest, directly in the mesh (the matrix of the universal whole). Alchemy has always been quantum, the Greeks spoke of a spirit that structured matter at will, *"mens agitat molem"*. Lavoisier and 18th century chemists rejected alchemy because they worked on the scale of the visible, but we discover that the approach of the invisible or the smallest makes two physics cohabit with different laws, as if the laws of one universe were not those of the other.

Indeed, it lies in the understanding of an even smaller universe where the laws of the smallest charm with malice the laws of the greatest (a harmony of higher forces disrupted by the smallest). Information flows do not circulate according to a binary logic of the yes/no type (or 1 - 0), but in an indeterminate or probabilistic way, which allows the notions of charm coefficient[cc] and the integration of a probabilistic logic with several states to be introduced.

Mikaël : So alchemy is also quantum ?

Doc Faust : To this day, the modelled quantum physics has not formalize the universality of alchemy, but the foundations of quantum physics help us to better understand a part of it. For quantum physics to be alchemy, I think it would be necessary to integrate new rules :

- ✓ The rule of autonomy (intelligence of light) of information flows, what some might call the divine spark of God that is in us.

[cc] Charm coefficient: in 1973, Burton Richter's research on MIT revealed a new particle with a particular physical state in the ring of a particle accelerator. Curiously, at the same time, Samuel Ting's research teams discovered this same particular state by performing proton collision experiments, then a new heavy elementary particle called "psi meson" appeared, proof of the existence of the quak charm which would be identified by a C for charm. Richter and Ting received the Physics Nobel Prize in 1976 for their work.

- ✓ The relative speed of light where the waveform determines the speed.

- ✓ The fluctuation of gravity depending on the pressure exerted by the mesh on the matter, the mesh being like a soap bubble interface.

Alchemical introduction through the middle way

Universe or Multiverse

God didn't create the world, he just played with bubbles

The world is a multi universe composed of bubbles where each pours its light into another.

Mikaël : So there are several universes ?

Doc Faust : Of course, waves can be emitted or absorbed. We are in the context of a wave phenomenon that makes universes as it would make new bubbles with each wave, the mesh being the interface between universes. Thus, the material behaves according to its universe of belonging. The multi universe appears like bubbles in a bath. To simplify, let's take two bubbles edge to edge, but surrounded by other bubbles that compress them one on top of the other (the multi universe). One of these bubbles is composed of emptiness and matter, and another concomitant is filled with emptiness and light. Nature, at the level of infinite time, and which does not like emptiness, passes light from one bubble to another until the absorbent bubble is saturated.

What is interesting in this relationship is that by passing from one bubble to another, the light slows down and becomes matter in the receiving bubble. Alchemists refer to the light of the emitting bubble as "*increated* or *original light*", and to the light in the receiving bubble of "*manifested light*". This light received and temporarily stored in the matter will push light into it and transform its shape. Some, according to Boyle's law, will call this low temperature transmutation because it consumes heat (endothermic) and at low energy. I am talking about energy reduction and low temperature because, with each filtering of the mesh or the electro-magnetic field of the matter, the light loses its heat, its speed, freezes and cools.

Finally, let us move on to a more peripheral view. We observe that once the endothermic absorbent bubble is saturated, it will in his turn become emitting and exothermic by pouring into the bubble of the universe next door and thus indefinitely in a perpetual cycle of construction-destruction. The expansion of the universe is then only the pressure exerted by the bursting of one bubble on another and the transfer of its energy in mass

Mikaël **:** Ouch ! I see the headache coming. But this reflection must be deepened since the apprentice must have his idea of the conception of the universe and of what light and matter are.

The rats bowl, church of Saint Germain l'Auxerrois in Paris.
The void is the whole, the whole is the void at the quantum level.

Alchemical introduction through the middle way

Doc Faust : Yes, but we're going to stop here because it's going to make your relationship with alchemy more complex ! And all this is only my assumption, my conception of the universe. There's no need to associate quantum physics with your entrance into the Hermetic palace !

Mikaël : I am beginning to understand that the secret is to get out of our heavy matter and, with our inner light, to find the meaning of the Whole. It's almost simple but you need the key !

Doc Faust : The key is clarity, harmony, rectification in the sense of righteousness and confrontation (or exchange) between the stone of work and man, "You are stone and on this stone you will build your church" this is becoming an Adept.

The Adept is in the mood of re-see-ving and per-see-ving[10], he is a recipient of light in charge of redistributing it to as many people as possible. You now know more than most alchemists if you have understood everything we've just said to each other. Catch the light and send it back to the world so that it may acquire more wisdom.

You can apply these laws transmitted in its time by the Buddha and so you will understand the allegories around awakening, the snake, the light, the compassion that it reflects on the world after enlightenment. But to reach enlightenment, the initiated will have to choose between good and evil, and fight against temptation.

I'm delivering this message to you, but you do what you want with it. Because willing to convince you would be wanting to own you and take the lead over you. A puffer will tell you about him while a philosopher will try to make you aware of what is inside you. The goal is to convey an idea while respecting everyone's free will. The rest belongs to the bold one who will make the journey alone. The end of the path that the penitent will take will depend on how his mind will be set on the cardinal values conveyed in our tetractys.

Mikaël : I have always kept my free will. Sometimes to my advantage, my intuition, which could be called "inner divinity", tells me whether I am on the right or wrong path. This, I know, may be related to indolence, but it is ultimately more comfortable and wise.

Doc Faust : You are on your way along the road you make. I would just tell you to enjoy the moments of truth because they are few in this world.

The bearer of light, Harfleur church

Alchemical introduction through the middle way

Mikaël : For the same destination there are no two identical paths, if we understand that, the path is wide open with its detours but also its shortcuts. Everyone has the duty to rise to his limits, the enlightened helps the apprentice to become aware of the danger, as the lantern shows the ruts on the path.

Doc Faust : In the end, it is the student's limits that will make him stop on his own, right ? The enlightened one teaches his student to go beyond his limits, which I wish you and others ! The path is the path, it is the penitent who walks on it. The path offers you alternatives without shenanigans, the pilgrim chooses his right or his left, aware of his responsibility.

Mikaël : The path is the same, it's the way of going down it that changes. Some dark men could also take the right directions but with a more obscure desire... Light and darkness are never far from each other.

Doc Faust : Ghosts develop a troubled soul, they convey an obscure message that poisons sincere travellers and then play the role of the dark tempter. The term is not the goal but your reflection on the path. Darkness is a form of non-light, it is not necessarily its opposite, it would rather be an occultation, a state of non-being. Yin and Yang do not fight each other, they coexist, they are in balance with each other, and this limit must stay.... Harmony is a relative peace between forces that oppose and cancel each other out without one gaining influence over the other. The movement of the universe is only the cycle of driving light onto darkness when it has taken over the light.

Mikaël : I understand all this now, but it seems to me that it is easier to succumb to darkness than to realize yourself in the light.

Doc Faust : Think that you understand only what you want to, and that often the truth is the manifestation of your truth. Light is not understood, it is lived ! Consider it without understanding that this Light is just here with its miraculous effects and one can be content with simply being a spectator or can choose to somehow become an actor of it. One day, while translating a Philaletes text, Henri Coton-Alvart was interrupted by one of his friends : "You take a lot of freedom with the original text !" said the latter. The answer was surprising : "I don't translate, I correct mistakes".

Mikaël : Hahaha ! That's how we go forward, we don't create much, we only add a stone to the building or we correct the mason's small mistakes.

Doc Faust : It is not enough to simply pile up sums of knowledge on top of each other without understanding. It's a bit like building a sustainable home, the good mason will take the time to dig a solid foundation.

Mikaël : The temple was never built by itself or with one hand.

Doc Faust : As for our collective work to enrich the MA of Nantes....

Mikaël : In his book, I found the chapter on the elements fundamental. I had already read about it but his explanations are more complex. The part on operations seems to be encrypted and it is imperative to have, beforehand, operated at length in the laboratory to understand it. Nevertheless, I did not understand the point about the Dragon and Ulysses, could the Iliad be an alchemical text ?

Doc Faust *:* Most of the mythological texts have an alchemical reality, they work by allegory, and as our friend Theseus would say, they are very good thread of Ariadne.

Mikaël *:* This brings me a totally new vision and I now understand why, as a child, I was captivated by the Odyssey. Reading the myths is not easy, I must admit, but the show "Les grands mythes"[dd] helped me to remember the subject and reclaim them for myself.

Doc Faust *:* Look carefully, there is also an alchemical reading of the Little Prince of Saint Exupery, Nordic tales and legends and even children's songs. All these texts are paths that illuminate the labyrinth. The important thing is to direct yourself on the right path, because I think that - and I'd be glad to reconsider my judgment- the philosopher's stone can only be obtained by the mineral way. Other paths are possible but are beyond my experience and understanding. To the one who is wrongly engaged, there will remain the possibility of making *particularia*, parts of the work or some medicines based on the vegetable or mineral kingdom. On the other hand, let's avoid elucubrations such as seeking knowledge in the earth, let's be serious.

[dd] Television series, co-written by Gilbert Sinoué and presented by F. Busnel. Broadcast in 2016 and available on Youtube.

The alkahest

When the chosen initiate reaches his creator.

Nothing more common on the surface than to define alchemy as the art of transmuting metals, and yet…

Alchemical introduction through the middle way

Doc Faust : Before Paracelsus[11], the notion of Salt did not exist, there was only the sun and the moon. What I am telling you here will make you perceive (pierce and see) the texts differently. There is in fact only the *solve* and *coagule*. Under the action of a tide, we don't talk about salt on the beach between the ebb and flow of the waves, it is a view of the mind, where salt is a fixative star.

Mikaël : Paracelsus used the three principles as components of medicines for all beings. But the ancients healed in much the same way with only the sun and the moon. The same applies to the alchemical work : Salt - Sulfur - Mercury instead of duality : Action - Reaction, Inspiration - Expiration. Paracelsus explained the three principles using the example of a wood fire : "Wood is a body by itself. Burn it. What will burn is Sulphur, Mercury sublimating itself, and what will remain in ashes is the Salt that constituted the body". Are the paths of spagyria the same as those of alchemy ? Amalgamation can very quickly prove to be a source of error in the understanding of texts.

Doc Faust : We can consider Good and Evil. We can tell you about the colors of the work. I think that duality is a better way of thinking in alchemy, even if from black to white we necessarily go through grey. The referent allegory is contained in Basil Valentine's "twelve keys", the king and queen are united by the sacred bonds of marriage, but on the wedding night, the priest doesn't play gooseberry.

If alchemy is not chemistry, I would qualify my comments by saying that alchemy is NOT ONLY CHEMISTRY. Ignorance makes everyone look for everything in nothing, but without nothing, there is no way to the flaming star. We can use spagyria (separation-reunion) as a means of action on matter, as a vehicle against diseases, but from considering it as an alchemical way in its own right, it is impossible.

It would lack the spirit of God, as our friend Pierre Dujols said so well in his Philosopher's Mansions (*Demeures Philosophales*) : "Let's not claim to imply that we must collect, following the example of some spagyrists and the characters of Mutus liber, the night dew of May, attributing to it qualities of which we know it to be lacking". I would also quote Ambroise Paré[ee] who said : "I take care, but it is God who heals". But when we talk about manifested light, it is something else, and in this eventuality it is God who takes care and heals.

Similarly, Paracelsus uses the concepts of salt, sulphur and mercury, but this is a poor understanding of universal medicine. Alchemical medicine is a "*Rebis*" a double and at the same time unique thing, the mediator having to disappear once the spirit has been infused. However, at each stage of the work, intermediate medicines also have beneficial effects on our body, they are white, yellow, red. The great secret of human longevity lies in maintaining a certain temperature in a constant state, the stone of the wise does that.

[ee] Ambroise Paré: 1510-1590 - "Je le pansay, Dieu le guarist." (*"I swathed him, God healed him"*). He was the surgeon of the king and battlefields. He is considered as the father of modern surgery. He improved a cauterization technique by developing the ligation of arteries, which he substitutes for cauterization by fire, in amputations.

Alchemical introduction through the middle way

The bigest mistake to prevent is to believe that one can move from the mineral kingdom to the animal kingdom directly. We need an intercessor, a bit like salt. We need to mediate through the plant kingdom so that the human body can react positively to the treatment. Only those who master the three medicines will be able to treat all forms of disease.

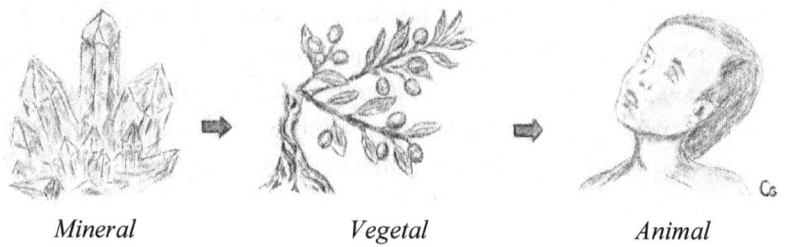

Mineral   *Vegetal*   *Animal*

So why go astray in all these ways of perdition when you can work on perfect medicine ? Maybe all this is a question of despair when the one who doesn't have Art looks for medications everywhere : in plants, metals, stones, energies,... Maybe they will be lucky with these poisons because "What does not kill you makes you stronger". But I must inform you that the chances of healing are as close as witnessing a miracle.

We are in a bubble that only needs to be crossed by the Light. Today's medicine is murderous and non-selective, it kills what's bad as well as good, no distinction. It is rather of the expeditious kind : "Kill them all, God will recognize his own", we poison the whole body, telling ourselves that it might survive the disease, probably. We treat the spectrum of effects and not the cause.

Light heals by resetting the system, it fights the disease as an alteration of the original message by restoring it. The repair process is like the caduceus' propellers, the two snakes enter into action and repair the DNA endings through the concerted action of Apollo, Diana and Neptune. The body illuminated with glory repairs itself, or more precisely it restores the flow of traffic within the energy crossroads and exudes the nodes of congestion outside the body. Nevertheless, the illuminated man does not compete with the l'axolotl[ff] who sees his lost limb grow back. But protecting oneself from illness and slowing down aging is already a grace from God.

Mikaël : But what is an alkaest exactly ? How is it made ? Can you tell me a little more about it ?

Doc Faust : The alkaest is one of the parts of alchemical medicine, and not the whole medicine of the last degree. However, the message carried by the alkaest can be associated with a series of original numbers, such as a universal, unalterable code, the fruit of creation, restorative, comforting. The root for this message is a beam of high-potential light energy. When this beam of released light touches an altered message, it restores the original signature, the sequence of numbers. As if it read the cell's root message, decrypted it to identify it and recoded it with its original identifier.

If the alkaest touches an organic, energetic and magnetic body, it will break down the obstacles to light that are diseases or alterations that occur in a body. The light will drive the darkness out of the body. Is not man's greatest organ his inner energy field ? Transmutation is

---

[ff] The axolotl has the ability to spend its entire life in the larval state without ever metamorphosing into an adult. It can also regenerate damaged organs or limbs. Not only is it able to reconstruct a missing eye, but it can also recreate some destroyed parts of its brain.

often mentioned but little is said about the other effects of the stone ! The other colours have their uses, their own possibilities. They allow us to observe the connection with the universe, the effects on the growth of plants, men and metals or the slowing down of disease and stoping ageing process... But the magic continues with reiteration, the stone becomes liquid and we find it in the realization of lamps of the eternal, the growth of crystals with the realization of precious stones of all colors, metallic glasses and metals singing like glass...... Oh and, I forgot, incidentally, the transmutation into red gold. But what I think is most majestic, at the final stage of the repetitions, it's when the matter returns to its origin. It is the auras of holiness that have always made me think of these magnificent orthodox icons where the saints are accompanied by the light of the heavens...

Mikaël : But doesn't the myth of Adam and Eve include elements that refer to the philosopher's stone ?

Doc Faust : The prohibition to taste the fruit of knowledge, such as Prometheus who stole the fire, is a warning to those who would not have the wisdom to contain the igneous force. Well used knowledge heals men, but their madness can have apocalyptic repercussions.

Mikaël : This means that not all men are ready to receive alchemy. Stories, tales, the Bible are usefull to remind us of this.

Doc Faust : A warning but also a -veiled - way to spread the wisest images and words. Adam and Eve who eat the fruit of the tree : is it not the adept who decides whether or not to take the light and complete his transformation ?

Mikaël : To move forward, there is nothing like going through the level of experience and observation. Producing a few crystals without experimenting would make no sense.

Doc Faust : "*In hoc signo vinces*" - "Through the crucible you will overcome matter and have knowledge of the secrets of the universe". I'm thinking of a test that I do at the reception, it's the metal penny test, not Judas'. To be received, the recipient must bring a piece of one of the seven metals to light simply by releasing the fire from below... I would say no more to keep all the magic of the ceremony. It is also a test that exposes the puffer. What has to be done will be done, or it must not be done ! Receiving light is very scary, going from word to deed is a moment where we question everything again. And then we say "Let's go" ! After all, it's just living or dying... The stone judges, either it puts you in a coma if you're not worthy, or it rewards you with new gifts, the axe of justice is final.

Mikaël : We don't always understand everything, we make our way when it is already partly written.

Doc Faust : The initiate must wait, be patient, observe... and then go for it.

Mikaël : Listening, hearing, understanding, learning.

Doc Faust : To know, to be able, to dare, to be silent.

Mikaël : The hell of a path, well, maybe more like a sacred path. A destiny not easy to follow but Oh ! so luminous and exciting

Doc Faust : I'll tell you that on the last day of my life, when I will look back at what I left behind. About fate, two movies come to mind : "The way" and "The man from earth »^{gg}. You should watch them. I wont tell you more. Great answers inside.

Mikaël : Where is the fate, the madness, the normality ?

Doc Faust : The madman is the one who is on the margins of society and does not want to abide in it, so we try to re-educate him so that he returns to conformity. What is on the margins of society is disturbing. The marginalism of Paulo Coelho's thoughts was treated with d'electroshock^{hh}

Mikaël : Fluidify our energies, harmonize our body, put our mind at the service of our heart so as not to alter the work on the path. Given my background, I think I've come a long way. I think that this book comes at the right time on my journey, in a congruent way.

Whatever the path and form it takes, what is important is the commitment to a journey towards the good, towards the light. You can be on your way from home to work ! Everything will depend on your willingness to open up, to correct yourself. The shape of the path is unique to each and everyone, the ease with which you can follow it will depend on your level of consciousness and in no case on the height of the mountain to be climbed. To be on the path is to give life to the material, it is in the purest *Companion** spirit. You are

---

^{gg} "The way"from Emilio Estevez, 2010 and "The man from earth" from Richard Schenkman 2007.
^{hh} Paulo Coelho stayed in a psychiatric institute, interned at the age of 17 at the request of his parents because he was "too different". He received electroshock treatment there.
* Companion of Duty (TN)

Alchemical introduction through the middle way

already doing it on your side with your pictures of stained glass windows and sculptures. It is a form of path that gives movement to inertia. Those who take the royal road are "extremists" of the way, it is neither good nor bad, but very personal and without any guarantee of success.

As becoming a priest while knowing that complying with monastic rules has never been a guarantee that you would meet your creator and become a saint.

Mikaël : Fortunately there is no guarantee ! Otherwise the path would loose its interest.

Doc Faust : The alchemical experience is personal. Who knows what you will discover ? Anyway, faced up to doubts, nothing will replace Faith.

The four elements activated by a celestial trinity when they point downwards, or by an earthly trinity when they point upwards.

The cardinal virtues

The cardinal virtues of the church of Folleville near Amiens

A virtue can be defined as an acquired, not innate, disposition that encourages man to do the right thing. Since antiquity, Plato has distinguished four main virtues. These concepts were later taken up by the Church, which named them "cardinal" (from the Latin "*cardo*" hinge or pivot) because they were the pivotal virtues from which all the others derived. They are completed by three so-called "theological" virtues to form the seven Christian virtues.

Alchemical introduction through the middle way

Doc Faust *:* It is said that the virtues on the way are cardinal and represented by strength, caution, justice and temperance. We have a very beautiful representation of it in the church of Folleville near Amiens.

Mikaël *:* Oh yes, I also discovered this in the Basilica of Guingamp, carved on a pillar : the strength extracts a dragon from a tower, caution holds a mirror, temperance a pendulum and a bit, justice holds a sword in one hand and a balance in the other. Since then, I have seen others magnificently carved in Nantes on the tomb of François II and Marguerite de Foix, on the tomb of the Dukes of Amboise of Notre Dame de Rouen and also on a pillar of Notre Dame d'Amiens.

Doc Faust *:* To move forward, no short cut to override the four elements, also represented by our four virtues, and then to rise to the three theological virtues of faith, hope and charity. They will very quickly be transformed into intelligence and wisdom, those who learned the most will then be led to enlightenment.

Mikaël *:* Enlightenment seems so inaccessible to the common people ! I live with so much doubts and so many questions.

Doc Faust *:* The work brings certainties, and once they are established, you put them on the scales to know their weight. But it is also worth making mistakes to understand that it is not only the truths that make you progress, but also the awareness of your mistakes. You need to remain carefull, to filter your judgment with the virtues mentioned. From four to three, then two to reach unity.

As in the alchemical work, you move from the original Chaos to unity. When you reach unity and only according to what you will receive, you will be haloed with light, or not. Because the initiate will have to constantly arbitrate between Good or Evil all along the way. You still have many lives ahead of you to move forward, this is not the last, it is a step, like steps of a staircase to climb... But if you make a bad choice at some point, it will stick with you in your future iterations. So hurry slowly because "*Praecipitatio a diabolo*".

Mikaël : I've been thinking a lot about the Tetractys, everything is becoming clear. Four, three, two, one, and thus achieve enlightenment, from bottom to top, from Alpha to Omega. It's all there !

Doc Faust : The invisible junction point is a transfiguration of Jacob's star, Jacob from J to B, like Joachim in Boaz that we see in the temple of some fraternities. It is the lost symbol associated with the lost word, one should not look for the literal meaning of J and the meaning of B when the truth will always be in the middle.

With the knowledge of the name, you become aware of the invisible and the universality, you have crossed the duality of right and left because you are at the... center. Hence the Royal Way which is practiced between extremes.

J ... ACO ... B

If you take the middle of the two columns, you have the word aco of "*acus*" in Latin, which means "*needle*" and which has been associated over time with "*medicine*" and curiously refers to acupuncture, empirical medicine by the needle. It's funny this notion of the needle that heals, a little more and we'd give it a color. White as for the famous Etretat Needle that we went to penetrate after

Alchemical introduction through the middle way

crossing at low tide this kilometer of secret tunnel in the most complete darkness.

Mikaël : The centre is difficult to reach, but that's where we belong. I'm following you !

Doc Faust : I am the one who follows[ii], as in the word Yahweh. The meaning is "the next", but also the one who knows, therefore who Is. Hebrew can be read in both directions, so it is normal to find a double meaning in it.

Is and Is-Not (*Est-Non-Est*)[12], the problem of communication between the IS (enlightened) and the IS-NOT (student) is intelligible by Faith. But we should already ask ourselves about the one who IS, because there are 99% of affabulators and very few real enlightened people, as I told you, they are a few living to this day. There is therefore little chance of meeting a true enlightened person in a lifetime. On the moral level, we also do things for ourselves, but under no circumstances to gain the recognition of others.

---

ii "In Exodus (3:14), when Moses asks God what his name is, God answers him, "I am that I am," he adds that Moses must say to the children of Israel, "He who is called « I am » sent me to you."

The Upper Trinity and its Four Elements[8]

Alchemical introduction through the middle way

Mikaël : Yes, vigilance is required, when we give. There is no need to seek to be known or recognized, no flattery, just the humility that lightens the burden of knowledge.

Doc Faust : We can see the Master as *Being In Me*[*], the M means that the Light has entered, the A that it is ready to come out like a Fire, if you cross M and A you have the star. First a descending fire, then in a second time the encounter with an ascending fire. We have thus : Flow (symbol of the Fire Triangle upwards) and Reflow (symbol of the Water Triangle downwards).

Alpha and omega, what is at above is like unto that which is bellow

It is the same as in the scale represented on the cover of the "Twelve Keys to Philosophy" book written by Basile Valentin, in which you will have fire on one side and water on the other, and when fire and water find their balance, when water is fire and fire is water, what will you find across ?

---

[*] Master = Maître in French, sounds like M-Être. Être = To be. (TN)

The wonder

Abbey of Saint Benoît sur Loire (France)

On the path, the man who is aware is very happy, even with the simplest event, because it reflects on him and his surroundings. Only the blessed can have access to the most sacred form of the divine.

Doc Faust : The path is initiatory and you will be amazed if you know how to enchant it.

Mikaël : Contact with a leaf, a stone, a tree, feeling the grass vibrating in the wind, perceiving the rhythmic timbre of the drop of water oozing from the ceiling to the ground in the absolute darkness of a cave, rediscovering the multitude of scents upon returning from an underground exploration, being emotional, whether in nature or elsewhere. The exploration of the abysses, an obscure environment so paradoxical to man, makes it possible to drive out our archaisms, to lose our bearings in them and, at each exit, to be reborn in the light. It is necessary to Be at every moment that we live, wherever we are. As when I take a picture, I capture the emotion of the moment, the one I will then transmit to whoever can appropriate it for himself.

Doc Faust : Even in a big city, these moments can be lived when you look up. Earlier, I noticed some beautiful sculptures on the pediment of some houses. What matters is to challenge oneself, to open oneself, to become aware of living in the universe and to be a positive Force of nature. The alchemist is a wonderer of knowledge (he reveals the *see it*), he gives life to the object.

Mikaël : Today, I began the visit of the Saint Pierre de Lisieux Cathedral. It seemed to me to be quite neglected in comparison to the all too famous Basilica built later at the end of the city. But in the end, this isolation suits me perfectly to reflect and take some pictures. Like many, I received a Christian education, but I prefer to enter these buildings alone, since I have long been removed far away from dogma and religious practice. There was a hushed atmosphere of serenity.

That's what I like, leaving the arteries too noisy and then, after a few steps... no more excitement, time here is set. As I discovered it, I imagined the difficulty of masons and companions of all disciplines, of those who left behind these amazing stone vessels, these messages hidden in carved stone and imaged stained glass, as a testimony to their art and their faith. So, how many hands have caressed the holy water font on the edge, which has such a deep patina ? How many faithful have walked in the nave and climbed the stairs to the point of wearing them out ? How many joys, tears and prayers have been expressed here ? The moment was intense, I was out of time and felt a fusion with builders and pilgrims. Sometimes I even experience a perfect communion with the masons by discovering the hidden meaning of their art. The emotion becomes palpable, the light from above manifests itself below.

Doc Faust : It is by following this path of discovery that you will discover that "*today's truths are tomorrow's mistakes*". That's what is written on my motto, a warning to myself as the fruit of my path. Nothing is ever safe, everything is renegotiated every day. Above all, it keeps you grounded. Humility unceasingly, so as not to succumb to the very tempting mermaids song that could flatter the ego.

But beware, life does not aim to accumulate good actions in compensation for all the bad things we have done.

Every word, every action is an engagment :

Alchemical introduction through the middle way

Today's truths are tomorrow's mistakes

"A long time ago, a king who destroyed and killed everything around him went to a priest who predicted hell for his actions. Panicked, he decided to change the balance of his karma, and overnight he did nothing but good, to the point that on the eve of his death he had done as much harm as good. At the weighing of souls, he invoked a fair balance of his actions between light and darkness. But his judge did not see it like that and said to him : you will be able to reincarnate 100 times in happiness for the gestures that honored you, but you will begin by reincarnating 100 times in pain for the gestures that disgraced you."

Moral ethics demands to be good now, now and forever, or there will be many times when you will have to suffer.

We have defined the moment when the apprentice works on becoming upright, aligned with himself and his surroundings, because very often evil also leaves its mark on our surrouding :

"A little boy made a lot of mistakes, his wise father decided to make him evolve to a better path. Thus, every time his son committed a wrongdoing, his father forced him to put a nail in the garden fence. Exhausted by these repetitive punishments, he tried to change and do less foolishness. From day to day, he improved even if the task was hard, until the day he lived a first day without mischief. But far from reducing his pain, his father asked him for each benefit to remove a nail already planted. Day after day he removed the nails from the fence. Finally he went to his father and said, "You see, you can be proud of me, I managed to take away all the harm I did". His father, by far the wisest, said to him : "You have planted nails for the bad you have generated, then you have removed nails for the good you have given, you have thus found a balance.

But there are still holes in the fence now, and for the evil you do to people it's the same, no matter how much you apologize for the bad things you do, you will always leave scars and bad memories of what you did."

Alchemical introduction through the middle way

Mikaël : Hence the history of birds[ii] already mentioned in the book "La Clef des œuvres de Saint Jean et de Michel de Nostredame" !

"Men are, in their relationships, as walls facing each other. Each wall is pierced with a multitude of small holes, where white and black birds nest.

Black birds are bad thoughts and bad words. White birds are the right thoughts and words.

White birds, because of their shape, can only enter white holes; and so can black birds, which can only nest in black holes. Now, let's imagine two men who think they're enemies of each other.

"Men are as Birds"

[ii] Adapted from a Sufi tale by Tierno Bokar Salif Tall, quoted by Amadou Hampâté Bâ in "Tierno Bokar, the wise of Bandiagara", French Edition : Seuil, 1980. Translated into English and published as *A Spirit of Tolerance: The Inspiring Life of Tierno Bokar*, Bloomington, Indiana: World Wisdom, 2008.

Alchemical introduction through the middle way

The first one thinking that the second one wants to hurt him, feels angry at him and sends him a very bad thought. So, he releases a black bird and, at the same time, frees up the space for a hole of the same colour. His black bird flies away and looks for an unoccupied hole adapted to its shape to nest. If no one has sent a black bird, no black hole will be available. Finding nowhere to stay, the black bird will be forced to return to its original hole, bringing back with it the evil it was carrying, which will increase throughout its journey.

But, let us imagine that a bad thought was also formed. In doing so, there has been the release of a black hole and some of the evil can be deposited there. Meanwhile, the other black bird will come to live in the other liberated hole. Thus the two black birds will have reached their goal and will work to destroy the Adepts for whom they were intended.

But once their task is accomplished, they will each return to their original nest, for it is said : « Everything returns to its source ». Since the evil they were charged with is not exhausted, this evil will turn against their perpetrators and complete their destruction. The author of a bad thought, wish or curse is therefore affected both by the black bird of his enemy and by his own black bird, when it returns to him.

The same thing happens with white birds : if we only give good thoughts to our enemy when he only gives us bad thoughts, his black birds will not find a place to stay with us, and will return to their sender. As for the white birds carrying good thoughts that we have sent to him, if they find no place with our enemy, they will return to us charged with all the beneficial energy of which they were carriers.

Thus, if we emit only good thoughts, no evil, no curse can ever reach us. That is why it is necessary to bless your friends and enemies. Not only does the blessing go towards its objective to accomplish its mission of appeasement, but it also returns to us, one day or another, with all the good it was charged with.

Doc Faust *:* That's it. I see that my words are paying off. I don't know if they're right, but they evoke good. I'm glad it reaches you.

Mikaël *:* I gradually try to wrap some light around my share of darkness, it makes me become better every day.

Transmission

*The closed book for hidden esotericism,
The open book for exotericism or secular reading (after A. Dürer)*

You don't leave a pilgrim on the road, you accompany him to the end of his journey. The teacher will always tell his student that it is something to be amazed at : having reached this point !

Alchemical introduction through the middle way

Mikaël : I have some friends who are looking for their way, the truth, especially to understand the notion and values of Alchemy. They solicit me but often get lost in insipid documentaries or misleading books. What can I do, what can I tell them ?

Doc Faust : You can help them if you want, but given the number of people you will have to make choices and take your time. Unfortunately few people ask themselves any questions. They have lost their free will, they follow instead of being... You will have to choose who to talk to because you will be responsible for the words you transmit. And when, with the teaching, the student has reached his limits and can not go further, show him that compared to the common he has already achieved the impossible !

"According to the laws of aerodynamics, the bumblebee[kk] has a shape that doesn't allow it to fly, but as he doesn't know it, it flies anyway !"

[kk] In 1934, in his book "Le vol des Insectes" (*Insects flights*), entomologist Antoine Magnan wrote: "First of all, pushed by what is done in aviation, I applied the laws of air resistance to insects, and I came to the conclusion that their flight is impossible." This hasty conclusion was probably based on the fact that the theoretical maximum lift of a bumblebee's wings is lower than its weight. And yet he flies ! His secret ? An ultra-perfected technique of 200 wing flaps/second, where each movement, in the shape of an eight, generates elevator effects, giving rise to sensor and nerve feedback that allows the bumblebee to stabilize and adjust its flight in a very reactive way.

Transmitting is your contribution to the building, restoring the truth while respecting the other. You must always tell the truth, it's easy, so we can never contradict you. But you also have the right not to answer or say you don't know. Knowledge has a price, that of effort and not that of money. What is free has an even higher price to pay than what you buy in stores. The price is moral !

Mikaël : Indeed, you're right. It's what I am trying to do because the fake prophets are always there and it would be much easier to be a clown like them. But we should rather try to show their contradictions. It is a battle of good against evil and there a long way to go.

What I give to you, your duty is to transmit it, while making sure you put it in the right hands. Write your story, our meeting, talk about our exchanges. The idea is that what has been told to you must be passed on, so that knowledge lasts and above all is enriched. The language of birds is not only the art of flying words, but also the art of spreading knowledge. It is also in the handover that you will find yourself making the most progress. You will have to help them, and being carefull to not influence them. Because people in demand are often vulnerable, you must respect them !

Working on oneself brings kindness, listening to others and that's already a lot. If a person no longer helps you to progress, it's because the student has exceeded the teacher or has reached his limits. But isn't that the success of a transmission ? If the enlightened one is humble, he will never pull his student down, because the reality is to see him fly. Volatilizes the fixed and fixes the mind

Alchemical introduction through the middle way

Mikaël : That's a good thing, it reminds me of my explorations. I had the pleasure of initiating some men, whom later carried out great mountain climbings or underground races, explorations that I might not have had the ability to do myself. It has been usefull to them in their daily lives, they have surpassed me and I am happy about that.

Even if we are on an unique path, it isn't forbidden to help others. I always try to have a fair word. There are three ages : one for ardour, one to get to know oneself better, another to help effectively without strength or pride. The trap to avoid is that differences with the other do not turn into ego rather than an ability to give.

Doc Faust : Well Mikaël, the goal is only to help you become a man who respects his own values. You know how to listen, so you will be able to give back and perpetuate because doing nothing is an act of disrespect towards those who have transmitted their knowledge to you. This is what I expect from you in return... The middle way is an alchemical and philosophical path that everyone talks about but few know the true meaning or scope. It is a score in harmony with nature that makes people live in respect with who they are and what surrounds them. We are just stowaways from History who should have done better by doing without us.

You smile, one day maybe you will become a Happy Man..... You see, words are already starting to transform you. Words are the Spirit, they rectify the body and touch the soul. Thus the Rose is born in the center of the cross.

In the beginning was the Word, it is the words charged with light that are the lifeblood of humanity.

Give life to your matter, make a sparkle spring from all these lost people, help without influencing, that is the rule. If the words of the other person change, you have put him on the path of his transformation. The hardest part is the first step, after that it goes swimmingly. When I talk to my friend Michel, the *Companion,* he makes me reflect what is right. There is nothing worse than stopping an apprentice a few weeks before his approuval, not because his presentation is bad, but because he does not know how to animate his matter and communicate the sacred fire of life to him. Isn't it said that a brilliant piece of art is a *master*piece ? The lead is where the mind sits. The mind is the conductor of the piece. You have to be honest in everything, even when you are facing a rejection. Life does not stop there, experience just shows you that there is a new way to discover. Or that you have to improve yourself to cross the obstacle.

"Dura Lex Sed Lex - The law is hard but it's the law " !

At the slightest inclination towards the dark forces, the duty is to stop!

Mikaël *:* At first, I tried to convince with conviction and arguments, and then I realized that it was necessary to patiently let the words dive and germinate in the other's mind. A grain germinates or dies, that's nature. A right thought must be transmitted with the right words. A difficult exercise because, if words are not adapted to thought, the opposite of the idea can be perceived.

Doc Faust *:* The phenomenon amplifies itself, synchronicity, causality, propagation, these are the laws of chaos in the Light, words are the vehicle. It is up to you to try, to correct yourself, because "Today's truths are tomorrow's mistakes". Glass is a metal with a high wear rate.

On this subject, the "Emerald Table" of Hermes Trismegistus is full of teachings, overwhelming, "moving" because what is below is like what is above... to achieve the miracle of only one thing.

Mikaël : It is crystal clear, everything is in honesty, simplicity... With the pressing need to follow one's intuition and let one's heart speak in all circumstances, in all places, in all actions... We have five senses, let's use them.

Doc Faust : There, you have understood the path of teaching. It's the same for a ritual : it's the magic you put into it yourself that creates something. Incense, candles, whatever, the ritual is up to you, just like for the path. It depends on your archetypes, it is up to you to feel what you need, the intensity you are ready to spread. You have to listen to yourself, not to someone else. Be simple, nature is simple, it does not seek to flatter your ego. In Alchemy, *"ego-non-est"("there is no ego")*. Only humility and respect.

Your first fight is to have your enemy close, because he's with you, it's you ! You must accept the fight of the inner struggle, the action moves you forward, you learn to muzzle injustice through the bite of temperance. White does not exist without black. You see, Mikaël, we are 99% of the time men and it is the 1% that makes us wiser. *"You shouldn't try to be perfect, but to be a little less bad every day"* says a Buddhist thought.

Mikaël : Each talk with you changes my daily life, like a spiral that gets bigger and bigger.

Alchemical introduction through the middle way

Doc Faust : The spiral is a very beautiful symbol, in the Middle Ages a cross or a spiral was placed on a tree or a stone to indicate that there was a treasure nearby.

The snail has in it the maze and its key.

After that, I have nothing else to teach you, the Master who commands the student is you and your path. You will have to orient yourself at the junctions and see the signs... Neither god nor master, I told you. You belong to yourself and your future. The divine spark is hidden in yourself so don't look for it under the ground or in the sky.

Mikaël : Gold is hidden in our inner lead or raw material to work with.

Doc Faust : It is the activation of the spark, through your work as an alchemist, that will start a great fire.

Mikaël : All these illuminated words take us out of the well of darkness !

Alchemical introduction through the middle way

Doc Faust : You know, the idea is not to be constantly accompanied... but rather that you fly as soon as possible with your own wings... fly the bumblebee that is inside you.

Without any pretensions, you don't need anyone, you can move forward alone without going anywhere else but deep inside yourself, following your path, and reading and experiencing the right classic books.

Mikaël : Your speech is true. You know me well enough now to be aware that I am strongly independent and that I know how to recognize puffers. At first, I scattered myself unnecessarily, as the seeker I am, it was quite normal. You were the one who told me that nature went through black to reveal the white dye.

Doc Faust : Since I've been talking to you, maybe you'll have opened your eyes even more. If what I told you moved you somewhere, you will now be able to turn the spark into fire. I always say that alchemy is an easy art that could be made by a child. For the philosopher's stone, the idiots have complicated it because they have given up philosophy or simply because they haven't understood anything.

In any case, I can guarantee you that everything that is said here is true. It is not those stories told and distorted but the things that I have seen with my own eyes all along my experience.

I help those who listen and would like to open up to receive. I would never seek to influence anyone who does not want to open up fully, that is the first rule. Second rule : do not sell anything, because profit in the name of our art is dishonourable. Let us not forget that it is a gift and, moreover, a gift from God. The reward is the work itself and you have understood that. When you are in the light, you don't have to say it, you have to see it, you have to feel it.

Mikaël : In any case, the falsehood we observe brings out the true all the more, and it brings out your speech even more. With its inconsistencies, an impostor inevitably betrays himself over time.

Doc Faust : What is certain is that the subject is only barely touched upon, because I will never betray any secrets. I help to discover but never reveal anything. I just make people ready to understand for themselves. I align them, I correct them. But without work they will always have to listen and wait.

Mikaël : The fake friendship, the fake alchemist, the fake speech ricochet on the deep thought like the pebble on the water of a lake without ever penetrating it ! The value of my work is to find and understand everything that has been passed on to me up to now...

The metamorphosis

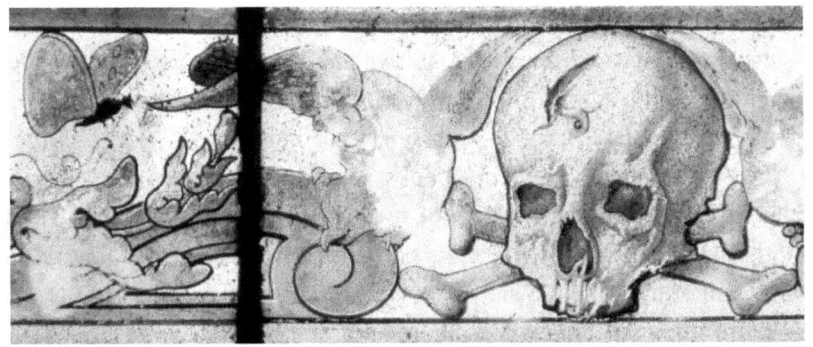

Notre Dame of the Andelys in the Eure, 16th century stained glass window

"To be intoxicated by perfumes, light and azure.
To fly away like a breath with eternal vaults,
Finally return to heaven to seek pleasure,
Here comes the enchanted destiny of the butterfly !"
Alphonse De Lamartine

Doc Faust : In the last few months, Mikaël, do you think that our talks have changed the way you live and see the world ?

Mikaël : Since we met, what could have changed in my daily life ? You're the third person I've spoken so intensely with in my life. First there was Bernard the philosopher, then Philippe the speleologist and now you Doc the alchemist. The messages sent were penetrating, I was wondering and there was an explanation with this simplicity to open the doors effortlessly as the truth can do. Everything becomes understandable where I was just searching and not finding. Previously, the few alchemy books acquired at random bookstores, the speeches of some..., they all seemed strange or fake. The words and sentences sounded like cracked bells. I could hear well, but there was still some kind of the impenetrable knowledge in all the texts. What I thought understanding in one reading was questioned in another. The explanations did not match the reality of the laboratory. I can only observe that it is more difficult to believe in the naked truth than in the lie that is disguised in truth.

Doc Faust : You know Mikaël, sometimes the informations are transmitted by puffers who present themselves as masters. The puffer is not a master of our Art, it is - at best - the one who served as a clerk to the Master in his work, the one who activates the bellows to maintain the fire of the athanor, the tiny hand who sees everything but understands nothing, and who finally draws erroneous conclusions from the sight he barely saw. When his master died, however, he was the first to tell everything he didn't know, as if he had mastered all of it. Anything he does not understand or has not seen, he sealed it as secrecy or non-disclosure. Disciple of... You are not "born" a disciple of... you are or you are not... you have succeeded or you are nothing more.

Alchemical introduction through the middle way

Mikaël : Sometimes, so-called "informed" contacts surreptitiously delivered me a few snatches, but nothing very transcendent. I was looking for the link between all the mysteries of the world's nature. Finally since we met, I have the feeling that I am more in accordance with nature and that I am able to create a strong foundation for the temple of wisdom that I must build.

I have the feeling that the alchemy came to me naturally, it was a logical following of my quest started a long time ago. This has profoundly changed my days. My walks in the forest become more intimate and my encounters more frank. But as a result, my discussions are more demanding, nothing is the same anymore.

Every moment became important, much more so than before, my symbiosis with the Whole became stronger. I feel, wherever I am, at peace and in harmony in a synchronous whole. The encounter of a mere stone on the way, or the gaze turned to the stars, these times have become unique, like a step that would prepare the next one. I'm a caterpillar who became butterfly.

Doc Faust : Your quest has no price, but the price is the quest... The treasure, rhyme with the number three. You must not find a single treasure, because once you have found one, you must remobilize to find a second one, otherwise you give an end to your dream. There are two terrible things in a man's life : To have a dream and never achieve it, but above all to have a dream and having achieved it.

It reminds me of a story... a Golden story !

Alchemical introduction through the middle way

A golden story.

It is 1924, the scene takes place in a modest room on Taillepied Street, in the old Sarcelles near Paris. Two characters silently work in front of the small fireplace under the mischievous gaze of a third accomplice (Perhaps Henri Coton-Alvart (1894-1988)). While one fanches the fire with care under a crucible containing a smoking grey mass, the other, a little younger, coats a dark, dense red powder in a piece of tissue paper which it then drops with extreme delicacy into the molten lead.

A crackling sound can be heard, like a fireworks crackle, red and green beads swirl to the surface immediately followed by a dazzling, almost blinding, glow. The molten metal now emits shimmering green colours and the smoke gradually fades above the crucible. The young man grabs the crucible with a long metal pliers and then spills the contents into an ingot mould.

Once the operation is completed, he immerses the ingot mould full of incandescent green metal in a basin of water prepared for the occasion. A long whistle is heard and, like one man, our three characters lean over the ingot emerging from the water. The alchemical gold finally appears, sparkling. The oldest of the three characters, using a slice, scrapes the surface of the ingot to collect some chips. It is immediately applied to mysterious manipulations on the table in the back of the room, strewn with test pieces and the most diverse instruments.

After several minutes that seem during forever, he turns around, looking completely amazed : 99.9% purity ! Maybe even more ! exclaims Gaston Sauvage (1897-1968), chemical engineer at Poulenc. The mysterious powder came from the supply of

Alchemical introduction through the middle way

Philosopher's Stone given to the young Canseliet (1899-1982) by Fulcanelli (Paul Decoeur 1839-1923). The third witness was Julien Champagne (1877-1932), an anarchist painter. And so took place the last known alchemical transmutation of the twentieth century, during which some one hundred and twenty grams of lead were changed into gold.

Mikaël : I really enjoyed reading "L'or du millième matin" by Armand Barbault, where he recounts his life of work and his work on drinking gold. It is a beautiful book full of wisdom and honesty.

Doc Faust : Honesty is not enough to say the truth, even if it is a good prerequisite. You should read "*Herbak Pois Chiche*" by Isha Schwaller of Lubicz[ll], who was by the way another member of the group of *watchers* who frequented "*Le cabaret du Chat noir*"[mmm] in Montmartre. You will see how the truth has many facets, the reading will be on three levels where you will always have to look for at least three meanings to a concept : the positive, its opposite, its allegory.

[ll] Jeanne Germain: 1885 - 1962, theosopher and Egyptologist will take the pseudonym Isha when she comes to Paris in the theosophical and initiatory circle of the Group of *Watchers*. In 1926, Isha married the chemical engineer and hermetic philosopher R. A. Scwaller of Lubicz. She will publish works on esotericism and Egyptology.

[mm] "Le cabaret du chat noir" ("The black cat cabaret") by Richard Khaitzine - reprinted 2018

There are thus a multitude of variations for three senses, including an allegory that can go up to five senses. Let's take the example of a rose : it's a flower, it's a cup, it's a perfume, it's a color, it's a season, it's a stained glass window, that's the allegory ! Look for history in history.

Mikaël : It is gymnastics for the mind and heart.

Doc Faust : The management of Fire belongs to you, I have nothing to teach you, just words to make you listen to. I give you bricks but you have to assemble the wall looking for the right stone and its binder. Leave your luggage and go naked on the way, because you were born that way and you will leave like that. That is the truth.

A path will give you a stick to support you, a *Mérelle* (Mother of Light - Scallop) to give you wings and a bed if you know how to cover yourself with stars up to Compost-stella. "*Ultreïa*" is an expression of the Middle Ages mainly related to the pilgrimage of Santiago de Compostela. This greeting of rallying pilgrims means : "To go further, higher". It is the expression of physical and spiritual surpassing.

«*Herru Sanctiagu ! Got Sanctiagu !*
E Ultreïa ! E Suseia !
Deus adjuvat nos !»

Alchemical introduction through the middle way

*« Lord Santiago ! Great Santiago,
Further we shall go ! Higher we shall go ! God help us !»*[nn]

[nn] Verse of a song from the Codex Calestinus (Book of Santiago) of 1140, preserved in the Museum of the Cathedral of Santiago de Compostela.

Alchemical introduction through the middle way

Mikaël : So if I understand correctly, it is the action of the ternary... who realizes the unity ?

Doc Faust : You see Mikaël, everything intersects, you already have a better understanding of the pictures you take. It is an intellectual and spiritual act to bring them closer to the work and I don't think there are many people who can or simply want to take this path, so you are privileged. Humans are essentially consumers, they pay for the right to not get tired. The truth is that knowledge flows but does not infuse.

But what I didn't tell you is that the more you move towards knowledge, the more complicated it gets. Doing, not doing, not helping... We go from material difficulty to the existencial obstacle.

Choose well-meaning people or you will be fuelling the wrong side of the force. If you replace light with force, you will understand the negative effects of light. And very often, it is easier to let yourself be tempted by the dark side, because these paths are faster... To sell its Art is something, it is like selling Christ to the Roman emperor.

Mikaël : It is obvious, the less we know, the easier it is to spread it. But life has as much beauty as facets, it is very difficult to convey emotions with words. The best thing is to live each moment as unique.

Doc Faust : From turn to turn nothing appears. Without obstacles, light can show its strength.

Mikaël : Otherwise, it's a blur ? A veil is added to Isis instead of discovering its colours. Nothing, tartar, chaos... darkness is in proportion as present as light. Nature does not seek to do justice, but to be just balanced between light and darkness, so that one does not take over the other. We are not only fighting darkness, we must respect the right balance, which also means not letting too much light in.

Doc Faust : To maintain balance, nature will make the darkness the most respectful of enemies so that a clear vision of light emerges from the well. Middle way, right balance, cohabitation but never control from one element to another, this is also true in your relationships.

Mikaël : Let's keep our feet on the ground, it avoids mistakes. Without forgetting to remain Cartesian, but with moderation to not slow down progress, one can then imagine a lot without believing in everything and anything. To be anchored makes it possible to have the immovable force of discernment in order to, with free will, enter into movement

Doc Faust : This is the message of a true wise man who is trying to give away. If mysticism is necessary, let us keep our minds and know how to live it in a world of logic without wantonly questioning the benefits of the world around us. Here, still this language of birds that is chasing us, in french we "guard" : "gardons" is the anagram of "Dragons". And the function of a dragon ?

Alchemical introduction through the middle way

To be the guardian of the treasure cave, the one who remains in the shadows to protect himself from heat and light, but he is also the Grail who keeps the light in its center.

The dragon is the base of the tetramorph which is inspired by the four elements : earth-claws, water-scales, fire-mouth, air-wings ! Some very old churches and cathedrals are built on dragons, "*dracs*"(demons), underground streams or wywerne. In geobiology we even talk about ascending and descending energy vortexes ! You see the oldest knowledge of the Druids has been passed on to the builders and alchemists. Never forget who we are, it is our responsibility.

Always act by weighing the long-term consequences, respect the right balance, never interfere with the divine will. Errors of judgment have consequences on our environment but also on ourselves and will be the subject of an appearance before our Lord. As God is my witness.

Mikaël : Yes, we have the ability to help or harm. We will therefore be cautious to others at all times, without our generosity torturing our souls. This requires real involvement, letting go of oneself, but also the possibility of leaving others in error when they persist.

Doc Faust : Everyone has their own way, with a necessary sharing at each meeting on the road. Because it's awful being alone on the road without being able to share and confront your differences. If everyone walks for his own reasons, there are always passages where we met others, for small pieces of the road. The mastered knowledge is intended to be disseminated so that it can permeate.

Mikaël : Being alone is not a panacea or a very pleasing experience, that's for sure. I have always wanted to communicate a "knowledge", a passion, it is our destiny I believe. So, during our visits to monuments, alone with a local volunteer who is kind enough to show us his church, according to the person I meet, I like to give him some ideas on the symbolism of this heritage. For me, this is the value of the meeting, the exchange that is created.

Quite recently in Minerve, in the Aude (France), I indicated the reason for the orientation of the church, why the baptistery is rather to the left when entering the northwest, the dark and cold side, or the reason for a very low door called "Gate of the Dead", to the south near the choir. Coming from ignorance and darkness, the newborn is thus baptized on the side of the setting sun, and comes out humbly bent many years later, towards the zenith, to meet the Light...

Doc Faust : It is the principle of the solar boat, of Egyptian God Râ ! That we find symbolically with the columns of time, with in the middle... the flaming Star.

Fusion of the rose and the maze of Chartres or the path to a smaller scale.

The ginkgo elixir

Ginkgo leaf with female ovules and male catkin

The flora takes its breath again, the landscape comes alive with pastel colours, the sun strives to revive the blood of the earth, the leaves covering the ground offer their putrefied matter to the young feverish anemones who will enchant the undergrowth.

Alchemical introduction through the middle way

Mikaël : Today is spring day, I went to a friend's house a few miles from here. I love this season. In their garden they have ginkgo biloba, the tree aslo called "maidenhair tree".

The story of this tree is fabulous. It is part of the oldest family of trees known to date, they already existed two hundred and seventy million years ago (as if time brought virtues to perfection), way before the dinosaurs. And because of its many medicinal virtues the Chinese have used them since antiquity. We don't know any predators for it except man.

That day, the purpose of our visit was to collect young budding leaves. However, we asked the tree for its authorization by explaining the use that will be made of its leaves. I'm going to try to make an elixir out of it, but I would like your opinion : elixir or essential oils ?

Doc Faust : Yes, ginkgo is excellent for blood circulation, it helps brain activity and stimulates memory. I like the sweet smells of essential oils, the leaves must be green and full of sap, so I would rather try essential oils, but this is a personal choice. Mine goes with my sensitivities to perfumes, but we can take the leaves in infusion or powder, we can capture the sap, consume the roots, flowers.

The male or the female ? Again, the question would be : ginkgo... but what to do for ?

I have another understanding of plant distillation, it is far different from books for those who think a little bit. So far from current practices, but so close to nature. There's nothing like using water for the first pass, then alcohol for the second pass.

Alchemical introduction through the middle way

Mikaël : I have distilled rainwater, is it suitable ?

Doc Faust : Folkloric water, I love the image of the couple in the book "*Mutus liber*"[oo] who harvest their dew in the early morning... But all this is just folklore. Well, let's follow traditions, but at least use mechanics for an unaltered harvest, without salt of course. You will collect litres of dew without having to run after the moon and reduce your nectar to a liquor. The ideal is to harvest the dew before the sun rises. It's more convenient than harvesting with a sheet. The best time is in the ascending moon, with the red moon, you know the one that whitens fabrics much more than the sun.

Mikaël : I have already tried to harvest the dew once as indicated in the books but I didn't get much of anything interesting with my sheet.

Doc Faust : What you need to understand, Mikaël, is that there are ways of doing things, but you're the one deciding wich ! Folklore can be fun sometimes, respecting tradition also means that you adhere to moral values. My advice is only not getting involved in superstition if you have to produce a lot. We are in the 21st century, witches are no longer burned by superstition. So technology, even if you are not supposed to be a slave to it, is still there to make your task easier and especially when it is monotonous and without much spiritual interest.

[oo] The "*Mutus liber*" or the "*Silent Book*" is a hermetic work published in 1677. It is composed of many drawing boards illustrating the process to be followed to carry out the Great Work.

Alchemical introduction through the middle way

For example : For ginkgo biloba, you can make different elixirs depending on the extraction method, you can use either hydrolates or alcoholates.

This means a whole range of experiences : which part of the plant ? What form of result ? What type of extraction ? What concentration for the solvent ? What instruments ? What influence do the stars have ?

A product alone or in combination ? Are you looking for an acid or basic reaction ?

Mikaël : Soon I will collect ginkgo leaves from male and female trees to make a union into a joint elixir. Females bear fruit not from seeds, but directly from eggs, in contact with a male pollen germination is immediate. It could be an interesting conjunction !

Doc Faust : The work can be done with a new interpretation of the principles. Considering that sulphur is obtained by alcoholate and mercury by hydrosol, from there I can see a succession of "*solve*" and "*coagule*". It seems to respect nature a little bit more than charring ashes. But to each his own.

Salt is a crystallization in a compound that must cancel the expansive actions of sulphur and the attractive actions of mercury. This is an "ana" salt, it has never been said in proportion, but in terms of cancelling two contrary actions. To be effective and keep its philosophical quality, your salt must have both the volatile mercury and the fixed sulphur to keep its philosophical quality.

Again it is the image of Saint Michael knocking down the dragon : he puts it in the ground but does not kill it, so he settle the volatile back.

Mikaël : Thus, no calcination of the plants after the extraction of their sulphur and mercury. During one of my first extractions, I realized that this practice was not like me, it was not normal, it was against nature. Thereafter, I no longer practiced this way, I no longer calcined or reintroduced the salt recovered after the leaching of the ashes.

The expression "*To make a perfect being*" often used during the terminal phase of "*coagula*" bothers me. Isn't it vanity to want to do better than nature ?

Doc Faust : Is God immanent and or omniscient to you ? Perfection means that it is both. This means that the human being can approach perfection but will never be equal to his creator.

The path of nature is a long and patient one, without abruptness. The rule is : if you treat roughtly, you're not a philosopher. So from the beginning with the ashes -in my opinion- you'll never do much. The work of three : Salt, Sulfur, Mercury as described for spagyrus, is a work of destruction. The work, according to my vision is conceived by the respect of duality in everything you do, Sulfur - Salt, Mercury - Salt, Mercury - Sulphur are much more in conformity with nature. But everyone has their own way ! The messenger must disappear in front of the message.

Mikaël : Thus the interpretation of the Paracelsian work would have become a work of destruction, whereas the royal way called the middle one is a soft work ?

Doc Faust : I am afraid that Paracelsus' work is misinterpreted because he spoke allegorically, with mnemonic tricks, but certainly not by leaving ready-made formulas ready for use. It's an argonaut's[pp] way... of an art Goth, ... Gothic ! A formulation that is easy to interpret but with good elements, a kind of protection so that the uninitiated cannot use it. Let's simplify, it's a code as our dear Blaise de Vigenère (1523-1596), cryptographer and philosopher by fire, could have realized. If I were Paracelsus I would have used good protocols but made with elements unrelated to the work. "It is so easy to make a tea with tea", except that you didn't have to understand tea, but mint leaves.

The symbolic representation on the cathedrals is a non-violent royal way where one finds the expression of philosophy and therefore of the middle way. No regulus, no vulgar fire ! At the Last Judgment the pure souls on one side and the damned souls on the other... In fact a rebis is the fruit of two extreme opposing things that we must bring together in the same place : a reconciliation, a marriage. Don't we say that men and women have nothing to do together and yet they don't know how to do one without the other ?

Between hell and paradise, the middle way is a road to enlightenment.

Mikaël : But then, if I understand correctly, to put the salt back, isn't that somehow reintegrating the impure ?

[pp] In Greek mythology, the Argonauts are a group of heroes who sailed with Jason on the Argo to find the Golden Fleece.

Alchemical introduction through the middle way

Doc Faust : It all depends on what you call salt, mercury and sulphur. Salt is a passive and neutral manifestation of a two-state form. I could even tell you that if you took a little dew salt, burnt half your supply with a blowtorch, the two halves would no longer look the same under a microscope, although they would still have the same chemical formulation. So how could two compounds of the same formulation be different ? The compound you attacked with the flame will not be in shape. It is the shape that differentiates them, the path of light circulation around the darkness. One atom will never be transformed into another one.

Mikaël : In Henri Coton-Alvart's "Les Deux Lumières", salt does not seem to be the "positive" but rather an element from which the original light must reappear.

Doc Faust : Salt is a mediator, a support, it catches and stabilizes light. Salt is a protector in any Way. (Saint Michael is portrayed with a sword, to strike, but also with a shield). Salt is also what unites, an element located on one of the scales' platters. The support for the action of water on the fire as in Basile Valentine's treatise on the Twelve Keys.

As I'll come to see you soon, I'll show you a luminescent alkaest, you'll put it in the dark and cool in your oratory. We will do a low temperature reaction without any chemical pollutants that would disturb your "dear bottle". The genie will be in the bottle. Then, you can tap a few drops at your convenience and fill the bottle regularly with white wine, the shape and its message being transmitted by propagation from atomic field to atomic field.

Mikaël : I will try my best to be operational for your arrival, I still don't know that much...

Alchemical introduction through the middle way

Doc Faust *:* But you already know more than a lot. You know that simplicity is congruent with nature and that we must stick to it. The Egyptians had little to experiment with except their intelligence and their gift for observation. So let's get to the core.

Mikaël *:* Yes, that is the hardest thing to accept at the beginning, let us immerse ourselves in simplicity in everything we do, as we progress. We forget to live happily, happiness must be a wonder on the way and not a goal in itself.

Doc Faust *:* Happiness kills those who seek it without living it. It's just a moment of consciousness. After that, when you know that everything is always fine, you stop looking at what you don't have to be satisfied with what you do have. It's easier to be happy in simplicity !

There are sometimes moments of doubt in life. So nothing is more important than to remember where you come from, not to look at the path to be taken but rather at the one that has been taken, because one day the path will stop suddenly.

Mikaël *:* A path is long and short at the same time, long behind and short in front... or infinite in front, who knows ? You have to live fully every day as if it were the last. It remember what you said earlier about Franz Kafka's sentence : "Eternity is long, especially towards the end. »

Alchemy is lived intensely, and we must be financially independent enough while preserving one's soul. Therefore, strive to do good, always "To be now" rather than "To have been". Material wealth must be used to give meaning to what we do. Money is neither good nor bad, everything depends on how it is used, it is an energy and you must have plenty of it to sell to devote yourself to the good for all. But I'm not teaching you anything about that, am I ?

Doc Faust : No Adept will pervert his soul by reporting his gold and wealth. This is what I can tell you : follow your path, the path of others won't suit you anyway. Putting your steps in another's won't lead you any further than the place where they stopped. But experimenting doesn't mean working without rigour, in the opposite, each time you have to carry out an experiment, you will have to carry it out all the more scientifically you can because this art is poorly considered by scientists. I really like double witness tests, one that undergoes the experiment and the other that doesn't. A bit like a drug that is active on one half of the population and inactive on the other half. It is the comparison of the results on the two populations that can validate an experiment.

Then, the same experiment must be conducted again to see if the results are reproducible. It would also be interesting to carry out the same protocol by two different people and to see if the conductor could have an influence on the experience, if one of the two protagonists could exercise his charm coefficient.

So step back, and do what you feel. Remembering that I might make mistakes and that we don't know everything will help you to stay humble and never take the lead over anyone. To illuminate a path is to share your own experience with your successes and especially your failures. After that, it's the next one who makes good use of it or not. You may be right and I might be wrong, it doesn't matter. There is no shame in being only a man like any other. Being aware of our's human weaknesses helps to move others towards the divine.

Alchemical introduction through the middle way

Mikaël : What a lesson of humility when I see all those who only think of becoming richer personally instead of using their knowledge to enrich others !

Cybele at the pediment of Notre Dame de Paris Cathedral
Cybele Mother Nature and patron saint of alchemists

Alchemical introduction through the middle way

Doc Faust : To progress in your work, you need a real laboratory. And ask yourself the question of the goal you want to achieve before you focus on the means. As you love to experiment on plants, you can steam leaves, water them, put them in alcohol, use solvents, work with macerated or freshly picked mixes, compare roots with stems and leaves, these are all leads... I do not share the same path, but my experience of the mineral path allows me to transpose its laws onto another road, which is just another parallel one.

If I were on your way, I would also wonder how your products should be assimilated, by which organ ? Should it be : oil, powder, liquid, alcohol, spirit, product alone or accompanied ? Be careful not to administer anything on anyone. The basis of poisons, like medicines, are found in plants. Mikaël, you are in the maze, and if you don't question yourself beforehand, you won't get out.

I'm sorry to be straightforeward, but you have to unlearn. You use your hands, don't forget that they are connected above all to a heart. The heart questions itself first, the hands act afterwards. Using hands alone is like the puffer reading a recipe and wanting to reproduce it. You can open yourself up to understanding nature on your own and not to copy it !

Mikaël : Oh, there is nothing wrong with being honest and direct with me, it will certainly help me to plough my way deeper. About ginkgo biloba, it is said to have a positive effect on the brain. I try to extract the sulphur from it, but it is a start. Each operation and test allows to progress on the method, then we discover the result.

Doc Faust : Remember to write down on a notebook everything you do in your oratory-laboratory. For neurons and the brain, ginkgo is excellent but useless if you don't evacuate the toxics beforehand, if your inner network is not fluid and connected. The issue of our century is in the accumulation of toxins that we throw at everything, in the air, in food, in the soil and even in our homes

My own experiences with heavy metal poisoning have led me to always propose as a solution a chelating treatment that starts with bear garlic associated with chlorella, this seaweed that attaches itself to all our waste and removes it. To this can be added coriander sulphur, then drain off all of it with hydroxy and energized mercury. Only then, once the flows are reactivated, can you take your ginkgo biloba elixir.

This is a good way to solve the problem : start with a thorough cleansing of your body. Now if it's just making a sulphur and a mercury, you can do that by distilling it with alcohol. Some theriacs are not taken directly, but are generally dissolved in alcohol according to Hahnemannian principles.

Again, it is not the quantity that counts but the quality of the message that is transmitted. If the notion of message is important in my preparations, it is not to be understood as an alternative form of homeopathy. Actually, on a personal level, I am not totally convinced of the beneficial effects of homeopathy, apart from the placebo effect of course.

The experiences are infinite, you could even refer to the first biblical texts where we talk about the tree of creation. I had fun in this spirit fertilizing a messenger tree with alchemical medicine and then biting into its fruits. It's beyond all hope !

What is important is not the messenger but the message, the quality of the information, and de facto its energy potential. It may have to be reduced or transformed from a mineral kingdom to a vegetable state, and then absorbed into the animal kingdom.

If we take the third order of alchemical medicine, where the message would have been concentrated three times with a factor of X 1000, it would be like consuming ultra-pure H_2O water which by its causticity would burn any living organism. The quality of the information is absolute because it is original, without distortion.

The real danger is in this energy potential which multiplies by ten at each iteration. A primal red stone already requires many dilutions and filters, what about a stone repeated in its almost liquid state... a dissolution of the body into nothing ?

Mikaël : I will assemble my two extracts, let them evaporate in the dark at human body temperature, and from there we can think about switching from vegetable to organic.

Doc Faust : You see Mikael, you have everything you need to operate, you have to do your operations with simplicity ! Buy the minimum amount of equipment, sometimes second-hand, except for glassware, which must be new and of professional quality as the risks of explosion are real. I am here to give you my vision that you will transform with discernment into truth.

Mikaël : You're right, I need to be advised that way. The spiritual advance is one thing, the operative is another, and here I need to think differently.

Ora and Labora

The man at work with his matter and hammer

"*Ora et Labora,* these words of fire sound like the ringing of a bell in the sky on a sunny morning. " Anonymous

Alchemical introduction through the middle way

Mikaël : I started talking about alchemy only a few years ago, even though I was already in this state of mind. Since I have been in contact with my alchemists friends, I have felt a profound change day by day, and especially with you who transmit a lot to me. I'm much more relaxed. Of course, I had heard about other ways of thinking, I had even been approached to join a few groups, but they meet in frameworks that are too narrow, too dogmatic for me. I'm independent and I wish to preserve my freedom to act and to think. Ceremonies and ranks have never really inspired me and I believe that they are not essential for personal advancement, but each has its own way.

Alchemy is what suits me best, a very individual yet accompanied path. A path I discover, step by step. I also know that the effort I will have to make will help me not to divulge my secrets with impunity if the wanderer isn't making his own efforts. It is the long work of patience that puts a price on the truth.

Doc Faust : If there is an alchemist who has laboured and persevered, it is Armand Barbault. His book "*L'or du millième matin*" recounts the sincere work of a lifetime. Read it again properly by questionning yourself on how what he has done could be usefull to you. Feel his philosophy, his faith, his trust. Oddly enough, it is the character who is closest to the truth in his philosophical approach while his operational approach is hopeless. There are very good philosophers with bad practices and very good practitioners might be very bad philosophers. It is up to you to find the right balance to keep yourself on the middle way.

This will open more doors, but ultimately it doesn't matter how many doors you push. Isn't the goal to open a certain number of them to

Alchemical introduction through the middle way

facilitate the path of those who follow you and who will pass them more easily with your help ? The Adept is a *master key* even if he does not make everyone pass through, he opens the doors so that his followers can receive wisdom more easily.

But at each passage, will you be able to choose the right door, make the right key ? And even harder, if you are in front of the right door with the right key, won't wisdom push you to stop instead of continuing ?

Mikaël *:* I think that progress follows our heart and intuition. Listening to the signs, questioning ourself at every step, but above all, trusting our instincts.

Doc Faust *:* Actually, you never get the wrong door, because what matters is not the door you choose, but what you learned between the two doors. There will always be another door behind it, that's the path : the end of the path is the door you just opened with your heart and what you have learned. Your past decisions determine your future decisions. Not by chance, but by a series of decisions that will guide your destiny. When you do an operation, feel it, if you are uncomfortable, forget it, let go. Let it go, even if it is the one of the other operatives. Always think for yourself. The operatives are also lesson providers who seek to have control over the others, do not listen to them. There are white birds, there are black birds, only your feelings can guide you by drawing from who you are.

Mikaël *:* It's better to live your own mistakes than those of others. You learn more by understanding your mistakes than to constantly repeat those of others

Doc Faust : Don't bully the plants, it doesn't look like you. When you heat up too hard, you reduce the field of possibilities. Your vegetable path is soft, do not confuse metallurgy and philosophy. If you burn, you slaughter and it has consequences !

Mikaël : In this case, I will always follow my path tuned with nature and even if I will keep listening to people, I will always think for myself in accordance with tradition.

Doc Faust : Yes, the naked man knows much more than the one covered in gold !

Crypt of the Abbey of Saint Benoît sur Loire (France)

Alchemical introduction through the middle way

For the readings, I suggest you to read the list of authors I have indicated to you[qq], they are good authors who have made their way and not puffers who will lead you into mistakes. When it comes to reading, the less you understand the work, the more books you open. If you don't understand it with a modest list, remember that it's not in other books that you'll find. It can also mean that these readings are not for you. Many called and so few chosen. So if it's not for you, don't insist. If you come across a book that attracts you, don't deprive yourself either, it's your path after all. You give life to matter by entrusting it with your goal, it is the path of an alchemist who prays for its matter which in return will well give it back. Help yourself and the sky will help you....

Purification begins with the raw, impenetrable matter, then the message is amplified by returning to the apprentice. The history of white and black birds is a good transposition of the relationship between a ploughman and his matter. One day man and matter are purified, man aligned and matter crystallized. Then appears our star, the manifested light that some call without understanding : Philosopher's Stone. It is true that the amalgam between container and content is a convenient shortcut.

Mikaël : So do we need to be aware in everything we do ?

Doc Faust : We are called to the laboratory, we do not walk through the door like we would go to a doctor's appointment. You don't force the moment, you don't provoke the matter. It awaits us and makes us understand it, then it is time. We seek immobility, the state of non-

---

[qq] See the list of recommended readings at the end of the book.

Alchemical introduction through the middle way

being, meditative, letting go. It is the heart that commands reason, then the perfect rectification takes on its full meaning. The philosopher's mind is liberated in the laboratory. Labore-ore, matter frees the mind, work on matter frees the soul !

Mikaël : It's true, I feel it in the laboratory, I let myself be carried, then there's a thread that appears, the alchemist just follows it.

Doc Faust : There is no right or wrong way to operate, there is the way to walk that is yours and in which you feel good.

Mikaël : I will soon set off on a long journey to the end of the world, to meet other cultures, I will try to find the alchemical meaning of their traditions, their customs. This will help me to make a link with everything that we have been saying over the past few months.

Doc Faust : Alchemy is in travel and encounters, in fact it is everywhere. The form of the message changes, but the message remains the same. As you now know how to think about allegory, you will just have to use their stories, their customs to adapt to other cultures, other ways of speaking, the language of birds is universal because phonetic and visual, therefore transposable everywhere. Universal alchemy is part of everyone's path. It is a gentle and timeless philosophy for those who know how to let themselves be rocked by their singing. The more you raise your mind to enlightenment, the more time seems frozen in you, with a universe in motion around you.

Mikaël : In the symbol of Tai Ji, it is the gravitation dots as small stationary points, that are used to contemplate the movement of the moving waves that carry « Shade and Light ». Someone asked me the other day, "What is Alchemy ?" Isn't it stopping time and observing the world in motion ?

Doc Faust : Because you become aware of the universe as a spectator and no longer as an animal agitated by the pack. It is the effect of the spinning top that rotates on a plane surface, but in the end, isn't it the plane that rotates around the axis of the universe ? It's a new angle. Is gravity a pressure on matter ? Is the speed of light constant ? In the questions new answers will appear as you go along.

Does the Alchemist get rid of his matter of incarnated light, or is it light that puts pressure on matter ? Light-Matter-Light, this is the life cycle of our organized chaos.

Front of the Grand-Place in Arras

Mikaël : This reminds me of the patterns observed on a front of the Grand Place of Arras, humpback and hollow patterns such as some metals that can be concave or convex.

Doc Faust : I have always been staggered to see that modern people always come to fill the coats of arms. Is it the fear of emptiness, of the unknown, of the unexplained ? These forms are already enough on their own without alteration, a revelation on our alchemical matters. One possible understanding of these forms would be to consider the representation of the mirror as the mercury of alchemists. Common mercury is also convex water in nature. At the centre of the cloud is the action of the traveling spirit that manifests itself on the horizon of matter. It is the gateway where light presses on matter.

Mikaël : We were lured into the notion of infinity. Personally, I have always imagined that what is at the top is like what is at the bottom and vice versa. Our world being only a projection of our consciousness, then to understand the Whole, it is enough as you say, to stop time and imagine being an observer in the middle of space, like a point in the middle of a circle, a little like Meursault in "The Stranger" the novel by Albert Camus, a character who is the observer of events during his life.

Doc Faust : Events impact your life and your judgment, the path is equal to our joys and sorrows. What doesn't strike you down makes you stronger, and the work becomes more fruitful. You carry a bag full of stones, and each one is a lesson that you transmit to the next one. You lift yourself up by placing them along the way, as a pilgrim would do, who meditate at each cross on the way. When the bag is empty, the pilgrim goes faster, so the more he transmits, the faster he will approach his goal. Learning and giving freely without intention is a blessing that benefits not only the apprentices but also the surveyors who, for each encounter on the way, will make less and less effort to move forward.

The harderst part is always to get started. Once you have launched nothing can stop you because, armed with Faith, you ostensibly advance towards enlightenment : "Ultreïa".

The first door opens on the quest.

The obstacle seems impassable, yet it is a continuity where the pilgrim will overcome the effort by learning to surpass himself.

Stanza and aphorisms, like crosses on the way

Stanza 1 - Alef

Transmission is a Work of suffering. It is practiced with humility and consists always in accompanying. The baton is hand on by so that a being in turn becomes enlightened. Opposed to the appearance of the absence of Being, only freedom exists. The pseudo master only appears and will vanish. Such as Narcissus dying, swollen with ego you won't be able to move.

The recognition of idiots will never be that of equals. But it is promised that the guru will receive the anger. For if darkness forces the enlightment. In the end, it is true in truth, matter will stop spreading. For the apprentice he must be like Yahweh an "I am" or will attract only contempt.

Sanza 2 - Bet

The light goes down like a magnet into the cup of the Holy Grail. The original light comes to be fixed in the spirit of the resurrected Christ. From increated, it becomes proven and then manifested. As light and matter, the Adept chooses between his orientation for good and evil.

Once the choice is made, it will weigh with all his weight on the scales of justice on the side of being or appearing. For his part, man will begin by accepting to die a small death in order to be reborn in greatness. Emptying darkness from your body to better fill yourself with the light of your origins.

Stanza 3 - Gimel

The DNA is a propeller to the sky that comes to life in the souls of two snakes. The first one fixes the volatile and the second one volatizes the fixed. Like an ascending and descending spirals, red and silver concealed bury themselves in it with emphasis. But let us keep in mind the caduceus who invites himself to form Apollo, Diana and Neptune. So that from three you make two, as from these convolutions the sun and the moon will be born. In the end, the alpha will join the omega, because what is on earth is like what is in the ky.

Stanza 4 - Dalet

The zodiac of the infinite is concentrated in every aspect in the crown of the announcement. When the angel makes him shiver as in Jericho, the veil of the starry vault will burst like a soap bubble. The border between being and no longer existing, will allow the divine to regain its form and, weighed down, to go down to make the land of men fruitful. The rebirth of Osiris by the Isis will be made once again by the buried bumblebee. The product is a glass rectified by the descending and consoling spirit.

Stanza 5 - He

All matter is a manifested light made of origin. Beyond the spark of a moment that stopped. The circle of space represents the full so that out of matter void is made. In a gushing impulse the junction of body and soul is made. Thus the liberated mind is set in motion as a force of existence. So that in endless cycles, matter is no longer an obstacle to light, but can return to its point of origin.

Stanza 6 - Vav

The dew is made in the sky. Its white smoke in the neck becomes black and condenses the salt into the earth. In order to flow from the celestial sphere and free the spirits. The Adept manages to fix the solar matter with his moon in mirror. From this marriage the phoenix will be born when the shell of the egg is built. For the green tongue to turn red, the ball will have to pour out artificially.

Stanza 7 - Zayin

Mark, John, Luke, Matthew, surround the green. The macrocosm in the firmament is closed to the ignorant, it will take him to break the seal, to find the keys of the two revealed books. The light of the creator is a blessing. But the veil must fall to descend and rectify us. With transparency, the veil of appearances will be transformed into an aura of holiness.

Stanza 8 - Chet

The master does not influence, he accompanies and corrects himself to show you the way. The "ME I" will lecture on itself, he will feed on what is small to better empty it and reject it. The "I AM" will appear to you in a tiny shape to help you progress.

Stanza 9 - Tet

Of a brother and a sister, it will be necessary to gather their roots. By the temperance of the creator the link will be consecrated. The tree by fire will grow. So that three flowers become fruit. May these seeds return to the ground. So that with a little water everything starts all over again as death (mutation - rebirth) is a pretext for life.

Stanza 10 - Yod

Emerald, for the one who knows how to take the step towards the ancient Persian language, it is the color red, which makes the heart and adorns the forehead of the fallen. Hermes, by his greatness salts his work so that the table is served. (green neck)

Stanza 11 - Kaf

The only answer you will find will be the one you know inside you. If the stories are universal, the experience remains truly personal.

The ego will tell you to believe, the free will will show you. It is the story of avoiding to put your steps in those of another.

Stanza 12 - Lamed

In Alchemy, everything is a question of perception in relation to one's own situation. Thus, from a small motionless point, you will find yourself in a universe encircling ! The immobile self will then be appeased in the ocean of adversity.

Stanza 13 - Mem

Lion, brutal beast, that at dawn must be hunt. By such a harsh nature and bestial appearance. Only water can make it weaken from its past. So that he can finally find his pedestal. We'll give him his sister to forgive him.

Alchemical introduction through the middle way

Stanza 14 - Nun

Phoenix of its destruction in the grey ashes, the bird dies at the bottom of a black passage, but the white moon brings its mantle of wisdom, so that an egg yolk can be formed, and thus the flaming pureblood become the most beautiful blood red.

Stanza 15 - Samech

From the truth a double fountain will be the source, white and yellow will color the work, only if the august old man lets go. In the end, the star will be the key as the link in the vault. So that the sea of wealth may flow through the salt and its water.

Stanza 16 - Ayin

The ars magna on the path of men makes from two lights a labor. By the infernal way only the tear will hold the work. And if the ars brevis is reflected in God, without any body, only the harmonic will contain the form.

Stanza 17- Pay

The *Prima Materia* formed, the *materia prima* will be hungry. By the celestial dragon and the water snake. May the passage of the two fires be sanctified. By the spear in the ground as the spirit of God descended from heaven.

Stanza 18 - Tsade

GRAIL, the man three times coloured and crowned can become a spectator of the glory of the spirit of the world. For the cup, emptied of its essence, is filled with another much more magnificent and precious one.

Stanza 19 - Qof

Two lights that will become one. Matter receives spirit. For the enchantment to happen, the miracle is to rectify the disorder. For this reason the void will become the full one and the matter a great void.

Stanza 20 - Resh

To remain silent in the midst of agitation, to meditate in stillness, to transmit to all those who are open.

Stanza 21 - Shin

Immortality is a time-proofed anomaly that will return to the moment with light continuing.

Stanza 22 – Tav

Student, you are what I was, if you understand me, you will be much more than what I am.

Be aware of signs

The Rebis - The alchemical union

When the signs make you aware of the fusion !
"The more attention we pay to coincidences, the more they occur."
                                                    Vladimir Nabokov

Alchemical introduction through the middle way

Mikaël : To listen to the signs and be attentive at the now, it is necessary to take time and reflect. We must be semi-connected with the universe between trance and reality. It is impossible to dissolve without escaping your daily life.

Doc Faust : Seek the spirit in man and the heart in the object. Be attentive to the signs, you are in an alchemical process, you must be in harmony with the places where you are, wherever you will be.

Mikaël : In the laboratory, I operate according to my intuitions, but it is always necessary to keep my mind and control the results obtained. In the last few days, I have been working there safely, as you remind me so often. I made seven elixirs from the same plants, made with different extraction processes. Then I placed each elixir in seven identical, opaque and numbered vials, which I then entrusted to two skillful people with pendulums.

The aim was to control the vibratory rate of these waters quite precisely without telling the experimenters what was inside, this work had to be done blindly several times in order to validate the protocol. The test also made it possible to measure on one of the elixirs thirty-five thousand Bovis[π] as in the evaluations made in the high cosmo-telluric places.

Doc Faust : It's always a good idea to use rating scales, benchmarks, tests when you can. Practicing alchemy without taking scientific measures harms our art and feeds obscurantism. Too many people

---

[π] See « Bovis scale » at the end of the book (p. 318)

work sloppily. If you go in all directions, you shouldn't be surprised to get nowhere.

Mikaël : Chance has little to do with energy, but it is hard to make relevant tests.

Doc Faust : On my side, since a few months now, the image of the last door has been appearing in my dreams, is it the final moment ? We'll see, months of questioning, beautiful meetings. *Patience* and *sapience* ! The creator's ways are impenetrable.

Mikaël : Time goes by but every year bring some surprises, on some year we make rapid progress, on others things need more maturation. We always want to move faster even if this year again many doors have opened. Time is flying without nature worrying about it. Our meeting is unexpected because it appears at a time in our lives when we are asking ourselves existentials questions : energy care, alchemy, ... those help us to find a meaning about everything we have done in our past, the light is at the end of the tunnel.

Doc Faust : The issue you will encounter on the way is finding yourself facing new doors again and again. People think that the number of doors decreases with the advancement, this is partly true for the tiny minds... For the others, we open one and there's still another behind. And sometimes, the hardest part is not the successive effort to do, but the simultaneous possibilities. The light at the end of your tunnel is just another room where you will pass and where you will have to enter into the next tunnel. As you have noticed, the only obstacle is that human time is much quicker than nature's. Time is murderous and brings with it a new learning, new decisions to be made. The choice of door is not important, but it is up to you to

Alchemical introduction through the middle way

decide whether you want to stop or continue. Continuity will be made with a new step of wisdom, so that there will be the transition to the other door ! Behind one of them, perhaps is the creator ? Mystery ! I haven't met Him.

Mikaël : The initiation path is never a race, I agree. But there is always the fear of not going far enough, of being at the end, hence your story of the man who has a dream and has never reached it...

*Learn that one man is no more than another,
if he doesn't do more than another - Cervantes*

Doc Faust : The fear, the death,... It doesn't matter. Everything beyond will be a recomposition of yourself, there is more than hope ! Eternally, you do the work again *"Solve et coagula"*. Maybe as the path advances, the time between the doors is longer ? That's a real question. I repeat myself, but eternity is long, especially towards the end ! Sometimes it's time to finish rather than to last.

Mikaël : Yes, the distance does seem to stretch indefinitely. As in the impossible quest of Don Quixote, a wandering knight seeking to reach the inaccessible star in Cervantes' *"Man of La Mancha"*.

Alchemical introduction through the middle way

Doc Faust : *"The Man of La Mancha"* is also an alchemical allegory, well, at least a vision of the quest : following the star, always walking.

Mikaël : It's an existential question, it's not necessarily a goal that I'm looking for at the end, but just trying to leave something for others, a last breath, a tear of hope.

Doc Faust : You see, what saddens me with some people is that they talk about wisdom, but their words are hollow, it's pure rhetoric to run a business. With them, the lie is more visible, and sometimes more credible than the truth, because dark matter is more dense than Light. Where is the existential consciousness of being, opposed to appearances ? One day, on the way, a traveller told me : "You have to be an I AM rather than an Me I", that's what alchemy is when it works on man. I work to apply this principle every day of my life. In his "Pilgrim of Compostela", Paulo Coelho talks about the test of faith when you're faced with doubts. It says that the devil's fight is, above all, a fight against his own demons. On the alchemical path, good is rebalanced against evil even if the hero's quest is full of doubts. That's why the tempter is there, feeling the soul of the weak approaching, he knows that the offer of earthly pleasures will make him succumb.

Time is running out, and it's frightening. But this is no excuse to shift the burden and responsibility to the other. Each being carries its own burden, surveyors can help to lighten it but in no way bear it in their place. So if you are exhausted on the way, maybe the way just ends there.

Mikaël : The next door will only be opened when the book is published. Next door, yes, but not the last one, because as in underground explorations, we always try to dig deeper, to discover, the slightest gap, the narrow gallery that will take us further, to detect the deep source. *"Ad augusta, per angusta"* or *"Towards peaks by narrow paths"* ... otherwise there would be no dream.

Doc Faust : The problem with the passage of doors is also that, after a certain number of them, we think that what we are doing is important and that we must not make mistakes. This may delay the quest. This questioning is a fear when facing the void that surrounds us, it is called : "Sincerity, Responsibility, Humility" in the face of Duty. But I also like : "Knowledge, Silence and Transmission".

Mikaël : All these words are full of meaning, to meditate on... it goes hand in hand. I prefer "Transmission to Know" on my side. Wasn't Fulcanelli's maxim : "To Know - To Can - To Dare - To be Silent" ? To can is relateted to "Power". It is a word whose true meaning has been overshadowed by men.

Doc Faust : Power doesn't matter, but generates "Duty and Responsibility". In the relationship from enlightened to student, the student learns from the transmission to question himself. In this act, the enlightened one tries to formalize his thought to transform light into matter. The verb is conveyed by the mind and becomes material through the personification. The word is no longer lost but recovered and the thought is transmitted.

Mikaël : In this idea, I am like the light of the candle, precursor to the sparkle of the fire that will fight the darkness.

Alchemical introduction through the middle way

Doc Faust : But to fight, a knight must have found the right balance between salt, sulphur and mercury. The elders said harmony between the corpus, the animus, and the spiritus.

Mikaël : What matters is the teaching that is provided to facilitate the transition of those who follow. There will be losses, misunderstandings, then rediscoveries. Finally, the important thing is the fertilized seeds, whose dispersed number will be able to make a plant grow to the fruit and not the seeds that will rot because they have not been able to find daylight.

Doc Faust : Even when the seeds rot without finding light, they are usefull as fertilizer for those who go out into freedom. You will always be more than you think you are : your body is connected to nature, your mind to the universe while your soul travels from temporality to temporality. An eternal future but not in your present form. You'll always have a use.

Mikaël : An exciting future, a piece of me on earth, a mercury mixed with that of the universe, a nomadic sulphur on a journey !

Doc Faust : Mercury is a state of mind, a message, for the soul to merge with the universe and the spirit to communicate with the body.

Mikaël : With what I have learned from the connections of Pernelle, I have a small idea of the afterlife : the body (Salt) having returned to the earth, the individual souls (Sulfur) are united at work in the great All - Spirit (Mercury). This conception is also suggested by the three principles of alchemy. In fact, between these two points of view, everything fits together and seems coherent to me.

Saint Michael knocking down the dragon at Saint Wandrille Rançon.

Doc Faust *:* Enlightenment connects heaven and earth, it allows you to be in the universe long before your end. Isn't it said of Hermes[13] that he is the messenger between gods and men ? The light that penetrates you gives you transient access to ephemeral states of hyper lucidity. These states allow you to feel your degree of connection with the creator, this degree of consciousness escapes all human intelligence, but when you return to your body you then become aware of the wonders that surrounds you.

Enlightenment is a grace that chooses you or not. It results from working on yourself and on your ability to help others, which allows you to expel your bad light (black light) to see the light manifested appear. Which happens to be the original light (white light) that passes the veil of appearances of this world. As with the cup and the chrysophea, you are only a recipient of this light. This lack of possession obliges you to a duty of correctness, justice, humbleness, and helping others if they are open to it.

Mikaël *:* This is how to start the journey, we get rid of our useless luggages. It is like stripping away a heavy matter with strength, care, temperance and justice. In a friendly discussion, we should learn to listen more than we talk.

Doc Faust *:* My advice : do not to try to persuade anyone. Using your knowledge to convince others would only be to lie to yourself. Where there is emptiness, light can fill you. Where you are full, matter stops you.

Listening is art

"On the threshold of the new door, ...

...the wise man should listen and will increase his knowledge. And he who is intelligent will acquire skill"

Alchemical introduction through the middle way

Doc Faust : Listening does not mean agreeing. Even if it is difficult, you can try the art of contradiction, the truth is at this price. You have made progress after all, hear well-founded and unfounded ideas, ask questions and give your point of view. The debate opens the door to evolution. It would sometimes be interesting to test the conversion ability of "heretics" and see if the new Mikaël is better than before, while remaining correct... testing your convictions in fact !

Mikaël : I have some educated friends, fine connoisseurs of history, French language and science. Filled with certainties, they certify that everything can be explained by the etymological root of words and mathematics. Their arguments are brilliant, but behind these demonstrations I feel a great solitude in their explanations. Why put everything in narrow boxes ? I try to simply explain to them how to see beyond words.

Doc Faust : The etymology of words, their roots that last over time and history, reminds me of Abbé Boudet and his book "La vraie langue celtique" (*"The real celtic language"*). Use what you have understood, use simplicity, example, allegory and historical or mythological references as if it were all just a game. You shouldn't think you can always go further ! Otherwise it would turn into a bad pun. If your emptiness has become full, your strength will be revealed to you, it will help you to use the meaningful word and the right verb. Neither too much nor too little, the right balance. Don't overestimate the person you have in front of you, and don't underestimate yourself either. The confrontation is then similar to a cockfight, but despite the violence, the winner is not the one who has won, but the one who has learned from his inadequacies. The loser emerges much richer than when he entered, which means he has learned from his weaknesses. If someone talks to you, listen to them. If someone asks you something, guide them. If someone has questions, help him to find his way. The greatest of the Cartesians is often a weak man who wants to appear strong behind his convictions reinforced by the rampart of science. Actually, fear makes individuals protect themselves behind what is established. Prehistoric man invented the notion of god so that he would no longer be afraid of lightning. In worshipping idols he thought of domesticating the unknown nature. All these self-righteous people are afraid of being questioned and your innocence destabilizes them because, deep down, the blessed and simple-minded child is not simple in the mind. A small flick can destabilize and weaken the humble seeker. And even if this destrution must not be ordered, it must be desired in order rebuilt ourselves better. This is called a "little death". Also, be carefull, because you don't always know who you are communicating with and how your comments will be used !

Mikaël : Intelligence, questioning, must be usefull and bring happiness to the other. Knowledge must never allow oppression. The candor and happiness of some disarm others. The straitjacket of education traps the heart and prohibits the possibility of breaking with conformism. The benevolent mind must break traditional codes to penetrate the body, some would say the heart.

Doc Faust : Our talks must be joyful, gentle, peaceful and tolerant, it is a step towards a new door. One door leads you with wisdom to another one, but without liberation, you will have to do, again and again, the same path. Draw on your strength to go further, just one more step. Because if the one before seemed difficult to you, the next one will seem desperate. It is a chance to help and not a pain, transcend yourself... the harder the pain, the stronger the glory.

Alchemical introduction through the middle way

Mikaël : If I understand correctly, I have to be attentive at all times, even if it isn't always easy. Not judging anything or anyone until I have heard everything that visitors have to offer. And in hindsight, assess what I have learned.

Doc Faust : Effort brings satisfaction, an easy path only brings laziness. You can lose a battle, but you can't refuse a fight. The hero does not die in the end of the battle but while waiting in harbour without anything happening. Being part of it, being invited to die in battle is a test for yourself. And don't get any illusions because every fight to come will be even harder and your feeling of isolation will get worse. ... It is the destiny of the hero. Receive the intensity of the moment each time to make your life an enchantment. The alchemist is a magician ! So when he meets an initiate, he sees what a wonder man can do at any moment.

Mikaël : Like Gilgamesh[ss] fighting Enkidu in vain, here is never a winner in a verbal game. When we contact the other, the miracle happens if different individuals can connect, talk and exchange. From the fruit of difference comes the embrace of universality.

[ss] "Gilgamesh became the hero *par excellence* of the ancient world—an adventurous, brave, but tragic figure symbolizing man's vain but endless drive for fame, glory, and immortality." *Kramer, Samuel Noah (1963), The Sumerians: Their History, Culture, and Character, Chicago, Illinois: University of Chicago Press, ISBN 978-0-226-45238-8*

Alchemical introduction through the middle way

Doc Faust : Plant a hundred seeds, put a thousand speeches, if a link is created, the magic will have worked and the miracle will be revealed. If you have a soul or souls to help, it's your responsibility. Comprehension does not mean forgiveness for the one who attacks you, otherwise you will receive suffering without evolution. The one who sinks must not take others with him !

Mikaël : Sometimes letting go is necessary because at times you feel the problems slipping between your fingers and there is no other way than to stop, to let your mind wander, to wait, and then... miracle, when everything seems obscure, a ray of light comes out of the night and the solution is revealed.

Doc Faust : Giving value to each step, further, higher. Be attentive to each breath, exhale (ebb and flow - *solve* and *coagula*), give importance to these gestures so that they become automatisms. All beginning implies a continuity towards an end and for the dynamic, after the end, a restart. What differentiates men is not the number of steps they make, but the intensity of the path they take between two points.

Mikaël : Sorting the wheat out of the chaff deserves a deeper look. You must leave the door half-open, as the middle path is not the result of an average between two extremes, but an investment in moderation practiced at every moment.

Doc Faust : Do you have a part of a shadow to illuminate ? Think about it, it is time to bring it to light, or as we have seen, to surround the part of darkness with light to give it a material form. It's part of your path to doubt. What distinguishes you now is that when you doubt, you seek to remove the veil. The nuances of lighting are to know how to distinguish between : lighting, illumination or blindness. Your constant questioning allows you to choose your fights because not all fights are to be fought. With humour I would say that there are three fundamental rules to be in the light : "the first is to illuminate, the second is to illuminate, and the most important is to illuminate". We must be vectors of light and use all our means to face obscurantism.

Mikaël : We are currently in a war of information, image and mediatization. Information has become power, disinformation an even stronger power. When it is associated with the images, it makes us see the end of the world. The strength of light is to illuminate the reflection of the shadow, and in the end it gains over the darkness a little like the transition from black to white being made by the grey. But for our world to exist, it is not only about opposing good to evil, but also about maintaining the balance of power so that nothing ends in the light or in darkness.

Doc Faust : Spreading the teaching received is a duty, the problems will begin when you have to select one or more elected officials. Why them and not the others ! It's inexplicable, it's fate, a question of circumstances, of affinity perhaps. If, along the way to Santiago de Compostela, you collect water with a scallop, the shell well known to pilgrims, you will recover as much as with a prayer. To pass on is to pass the baton, as the Greeks did in the stadiums, by offering the flame to others. It is a about the ability to open up, to connect with the words of others and make them resonate positively in oneself, to transform them into words of truth.

Symbolic connexion

St James shell also called Scallop

The scallop symbolizes fertility and expresses the convergence of all paths. It evokes our inner quest towards a single point : our centre. Then, after all the instincts of our raw material have been mastered from skinning to revelations, the new man can be born...

Alchemical introduction through the middle way

Mikaël : With Pernelle, we are used to, or at least aspire to, place a shell in the high places we visit. Soon we will deposit one at the end of the world and try to locate it in a place where it will be protected for at least a few centuries.

Doc Faust : Pilgrims often took complete shells with both sides, drew a circle of strength in their enclosure and buried them fan-shaped in the north until they left. They took the earth as a witness and with the influence of the rising moon charged their shells with energy. The shell is a kind of attractive magnet when the curved part is placed upwards (anchoring with the place as the earth and fire would do). But, if we want to energize the water with air and storing the magnetic electron, as for the holy water, the curved part of the scallop will be buried downwards.

We are in a direct application of Henri Coton-Alvart's theory, as if we were approaching two atoms until they touch each other. Then a bond is created, a message, a positive energy passes from one to the other. If we move these two atoms away to infinity, information continues to flow regardless of the distance. For the two parts of your scallop, it's the same, the two parts, when put in two distant places will continue to communicate.

Mikaël : Lately we have been to "Port en Bessin", one of the major shell fishing ports, in order to do so. Shells are opened right there and the scallops (with roe removed) are sold directly at the fish market. The opened shells are thrown nearby along the wharf. My half (I am talking here about the one that accompanies me for every day of my life, as we are the two parts of the shell or as Nicolas Flamel and Pernelle were) had the pleasure of discovering a complete one among the thousands of specimens, so when we returned we put it in the ground under the laboratory. We will only take out the bulging part three days before our departure on our trip in order to bury it again in another place that resonates with our senses and happens to be Easter Island. Even far away, they will both be placed in the same orientation and will most likely have an affinity despite their distance.

Groove are commonly observed on the chalk walls of Norman churches, these deep incisions were made with a knife by passing pilgrims taking a little stone from each church and mixing it with their drink or collecting it in a purse. In this spirit, we will bring soil from here and bring soil from the island, from where the shell will be, and mix it, when we return, with the flat part left in the land of France. This is the ritual we have established to maintain a strong relationship with certain particular places charged with the energy of the place, a little like in space, where time passes through wormholes to move from one point of space and time to another. The symbolism we are creating here is the same. What's up is like what's down.

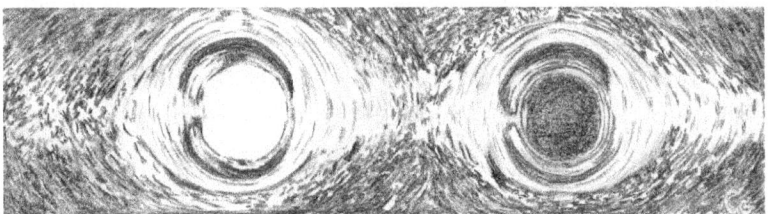

Doc Faust : Lady Pernelle has collected the only complete shell, it is a sign. They are triggered when you set out on the way, it is not a coincidence. Chance is a destiny covered with stars organized according to the path to be followed and shows to attentive eyes the direction to follow.

What you have done here is highly symbolic, you have transposed the theory of quantum connection with a ritual specific to you. You have chosen your path without following in someone else's footsteps but still by using the laws that the surveyor has given you. You have just woven a link between two doors on the way, well that's some wonders on your way. Thus Schrödinger, one of the founding fathers of quantum physics, explained that two intertwined particles, brought into contact and then infinitely distant, form a single system of solidarity in space and time. The relationship between them is unalterable (Einstein will speak of ghostly action at a distance) and when one of the particles is measured, the same measurement is found on the other particle. If we continue our analogy between entanglement and alchemy, the more objects you place between two or more places, the more vortexes (paths, wormholes, you weave communicating between the objects and the places. It is the image of a spider that is placed in the center of its web and captures each of the peripheral vibrations.

Mikaël : In 1935, Einstein did not want to admit this phenomenon of connection faster than the speed of light because it was in total contradiction with his theory of restricted relativity. Then, in 1982, Alain Aspect carried out some experiments on pairs of photons. When he separated two, one reacted simultaneously with the other despite the distance separating them. This made it possible to verify the entanglement laws, and the non-local aspect attributed to the quantum. These results, which have since been validated by other physicists, flout the order established by traditional physics. We can imagine that photons are part of a global reality and give a holistic character to space.

According to this idea, I wonder if the alkaest wouldn't allow me to connect to the frame by magnifying this moment ?

Doc Faust : If alkaest is mostly a theriac that cures many diseases, it also allows you to realize mystical and quantum singularities. As in any experiment, take note. There will inevitably be small signs that will make you distinguish between the realm of chance and the realm of the startling. In any case, be attentive because there will be many anomalies to interpret during your trip, I can feel it ! But will you know how to open yourself up enough to capture what it is and what it means ? This approach is very symbolic and is in accordance to your way of doing things. You create links between your home and the sites that inspire you, it's a bit like drawing rays of light between the sun and its mirror star. You seek the complicity or even the complementarity of places, situations and actors. As for the three medicines, they have an energetic impact on your body and a spiritual action on your soul and body. Some incurable patients were able to survive very long after the absorption of adequate medicine, to the great displeasure (*damnum*) of some doctors who, instead of facing what is beyond them, immediately awarded the miracle of their talent. I still remember someone who doctors had given up hope on, as he had generalized cancer with metastases that gnawed at his bones to the point of being visible on X-ray. After treatment, here is this man, a doctor moreover, taking over the disease, and sees it completely disappear after a few months and, as a bonus, to find a bone structure free of any stigma. Well, annoyed by his total recovery, this miraculous doctor, told smilling to the incredulous medical profession that he was a strong believer and had never stopped praying in Lourdes !

From black to white

Many men unravel, few men die
"The Abyss" by M. Yourcenar (French Title "L'œuvre au noir")

"Each of us is his only master and his only adept. The experience is repeated each time from scratch."
Excerpt from "The Abyss" by Marguerite Yourcenar, 1968.

Mikaël : The tool is an extension of the hand, and not a *modus operandi* that the artist must follow, because looking too much through the camera's viewfinder... we forget to watch life pass !

During my shots, I often make a quick general passage, then a series of more in-depth photos, then a new passage by living the present moment and widening my vision.

I never look up on the internet or books before visiting a monument, I watch and discover intuitively step by step.

Doc Faust : So you see without interference, with intuition, with the feeling of your five senses. I should even say your six senses now that you have been initiated with Christic oil. Despite a more promising path than some others, you will have to keep the respect of the elders. Everyone has their own vision of the path.

Mikaël : I read the stories of explorers at the beginning of the century, willing to follow in their footsteps. I happily followed their spirit but not, fortunately for me, the rudimentary way of doing things that was inherent in their time.

Doc Faust : Understanding also means respecting the journey of others and capitalizing on the results of their experience. To place one's steps in those of another is what puffers who claim to be alchemists do : it is a dead end. But observing the manifestations that result from a path taken by a soul with a light heart always makes it possible to learn about oneself, whether the other's experience has been good or bad.

An apprentice alchemist worked on his furnace for thirty years, day after day and without respite. It melted and cooled its antimony continuously for years until one day, during a fusion, the metal became transparent. This man, who found his gold without becoming a follower, found his way to happiness. You don't have to be an adept to find happiness.

Mikaël : What legitimacy do some people have to give advice to everyone around when humbleness pushes you to stay in the shadows ? To be without showing off requires, for the one who wants to learn, passing through a test of faith.

Faith is one thing, as the adept who shows his pupil a transmutation will be rare, but faith cannot guide you all along the way without witnessing the manifestation. Also from blind, it is always interesting to become a Saint Thomas.

Books don't help to carry out the work, as those who wrote them only gave the testimony of who they were. But, when interpreted correctly, clues help the reader to move forward. Suffering isn't as a labyrinth, but a hint at the junction of a path.

There is a thin line between those who use knowledge wisely and those who use it as a tool to gain power over others. A bit like the church which believe it is invested with the power of God on earth and divert our sacred places and our believers.

Mikaël : Beautiful words convert those whose spirit is weak, too many seek to be honoured, even in the world of alchemy. As a young man, I already felt the quests for power of some scientists over their other colleagues, it enlightened me, sometimes amused, and often annoyed.

Doc Faust : Just because you are illuminated on one path does not mean that another path won't also be enlighted. There are many ways to go, but they must be followed with sincerity. Several sources can either drown you or strengthen you when you have to swim in the flow.

The path is like a river, if he stands still in front of the obstacle, the water is disturbed by the current, but if the penitent moves at the same speed as the flow, the same water becomes transparent. The result of the work is an ability to walk faster to see more transparency in this moving water.

Mikaël : But multiplying the sources could also mean getting lost ?

Doc Faust : All these tumultuous tides are calmed down by forming larger, less spectacular streams, but ultimately more powerful. Thus the foundation of a good initiation is not to buy a multitude of books, understanding the meaning of the first one means that you are simply ready to walk through a new door.

We have to look in a strong current, searching for the origin of knowledge coming from the smallest source.

But don't worry, whatever your degree of initiation and progress is, nature is infinite in its desires and man limited in his possibilities. We will all have a last closed door in front of which we will stop, time is running out and fortunately spirituality is not a race.

To be immersed in the truth is to get at the last door as a man happy with the path accomplished and not saddened with the one we will not open.

Alchemical introduction through the middle way

Mikaël : We must not fool ourselves believing that what we are more that we are, and under no circumstances believe that surpassing ourselves has no limits.

Doc Faust : Even the most spiritually evolved being is only a sum of imperfections. His distance from the apprentice must not lead the seeker to believe that he is hiding truths from him. The enlightened is imperfect, to teach he must put on his habit of imperfections and do the best he can. The truth in all this is that it is not for the enlightened to look like a perfect human being, but for the student to accept what is. We see a ray of light much better if we are placed in the dark.

Mikaël : Black is the first test to pass, man is therefore at the opposite of God. All the work consists in reducing this distance and moving to perfect transparency. It is like caving, the most deserving, the one who will learn the most, is not the first one reaching the bottom of the abyss but the last one who will have suffered a lot to get there by helping others to do better.

Doc Faust : Black is an awareness of who you are and what you no longer want to be, so the movement to go white is triggered. This little death is an opportunity to be reborn.

I had a contact in the last few days with someone who told me he knew you, that you were talking to him about philosophy and alchemical tradition. I'm glad you're moving on to other traditions. Alchemy has never been the science of power over the other, but the science of passage according to the tradition of information.

Mikaël : He was going into a dead end or rather into a long maze. You told me that I could in my turn spread some useful information.

Alchemical introduction through the middle way

I gave him the first good elements to study and move forward so that he could discover his way without getting lost.

I transmit the spirit, words are only the bearers. It is essential to pass over words in order to understand their spirit. This allows us to remember that even if we are draw into the celestial spheres, we are still earthly beings.

Doc Faust : So he should start by unlearning. But beware, do not teach anyone, choose the messenger carefully, see if time makes him a worthy being, because without the right sentence, the verb could be lost again (*Verbum demissum*).

Mikaël : Obviously, if I see that a person is sincerely looking and asking me for directions, I take them on a visit to a monument, a book or an image. Then I observe the man according to his questions much more than with the expression of his answers.

If I detect the man in quest, I continue, a little like on a mountain expedition. We see the personality over the duration of the event, I accompany the man who will be judged by the mountain.

Doc Faust : Nature is an amazing trial. In another time, God's judgment was used in a conflict between two people.

In hiking you can see very quickly whoever continues the path as in a sprint or as in a marathon.

Mikaël : We will leave as planned, to the end of the world, in the next few days. I will try to communicate with you from there as much as I can....

Doc Faust : Don't forget the scallop ! Because what you are about to achieve will be highly symbolic, initiatory and emotional for you. Weave the link, you'll see if it's still there when you will come back. In any case, one never emerges unscathed from trials and journeys, perhaps stronger, rarely weaker, but always transformed.

Mikaël : I extracted it yesterday. I assimilated a few drops of alkaest, and I had then fever all night and some strange dreams...

Doc Faust : Yes, the symptom is familiar. You cleanse your body to receive the spirit. Have a good trip, both of you, and see you soon, God willing !

The initiatory journey

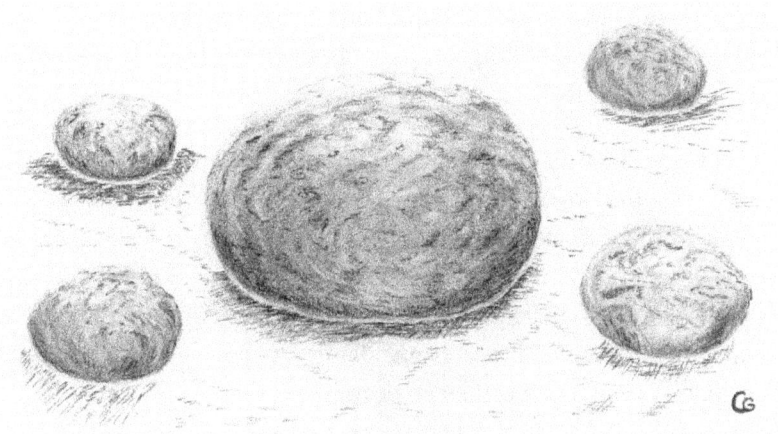

"The navel of the world" or the Mana Stone from Easter Island [14]. It is surrounded by four stones representing the four cardinal points.

"I am a traveller and navigator, and every day I discover a new continent in the depths of my soul"

Khalil Gibran

Alchemical introduction through the middle way

Mikaël : We arrived recently, communication with the Western world is not easy in these southern lands. We sometimes stay on islands in the Pacific Ocean that have no electricity or running water, so we live off with the water from the sky, fruits and fishing. Our exchanges with the locals are great, everything is easy. No "Me I", no "I have", every word expresses peace, wisdom, even love. Everyone turns around to greet us with a word, a friendly gesture, to offer us a fruit, a fish.

We don't necessarily talk, we look at each other, the eyes are enough to express the joy of meeting each other. Moreover, when we memorize these moments with a picture, our newest friend closes his eyes modestly in order to internalize the moment forever, the face exhales serenity, there is a certain exchange of affection, it is unimaginable. The embrace is mandatory at each separation and the connexion of the looks is then so deep...

I realize why Bougainville named these islands "The New Kythira".

Doc Faust : Only the body emptied of mind let you learn, even in these countries. As nothing will sink in if you're already full ! Words are water pearls and sentences are wakes. As our poet friend Joachim Du Bellay made us discover in his time.

"Happy who, like Odysseus, has made a beautiful journey,

Or as the one who conquered the fleece,

And then returned, full of experience and reason,

Living with his parents for the rest of his life ! »

Alchemical introduction through the middle way

Mikaël : I already came, twice in this part of the world, but now after a few years of travelling on my way, of following a teaching, I feel my sensitivity enhanced in these encounters. Here, nothing artificial, nothing superficial, no oversized ego.

Men have, like everyone else in the world, their qualities and defects, but the magic of the heart is so visible.

There is a real soul to soul complicity. I didn't thought I had reached this point of perception.

Doc Faust : It's usual, alchemy has made you wiser, you're ready to receive ! Like a magnet.

Mikaël : Everyone here knows the names of the trees and flowers, in French and Tahitian. Each tree, each place has its own history, its own legend, its own ancestor, its own archetypes. I used to talk about mythology, Egyptian, Greek or Roman, and there we discover a wonderful mythology close to the primary gods and nature. There are many similarities with our mythology about cosmogony, or the creation of man and woman. But here all this still seems very much alive, probably thanks to this oral tradition that conveys emotion better.

We are lucky because we stay with elders, they know the medicinal properties of each plant. We have made remedies based on coconut and noni, including a purge to be absorbed by the pregnant woman in the seventh and eighth months of pregnancy so that the baby is born clean both outside and inside. The placenta will be collected by the father and placed in the ground at the foot of a young coconut tree shoot planted for the occasion at the very top of the mountain. A true alchemical connection between men and gods, between plants, the land of ancestors and heaven.

Doc Faust *:* The language of gods is universal. You will feel the depth of the words, you will understand them without having to translate them by their intensity, the language of birds is universal, it assists knowledge thanks to the metaphor.

Mickaël : Yes, that's what I feel too. I understand and still don't know how this is possible. We understand the messages of the spirit transmitted to our senses !

Doc Faust *:* You bet, it's an intense experience when you're connected.

Connexity with Easter Island

Moaï in the quarry of Rano Raraku on Easter Island

Te Pito O Te Henua or Easter Island, a small volcanic island lost in the vastness of the Pacific Ocean which feverishly projects its jagged flanks into the sky... There is a singular atmosphere here, the history of the particular statues and of its people so admirable, the perfumes, the horses in freedom, the colours of the blond grass swept by the wind.

Alchemical introduction through the middle way

Our journey continues across the Pacific, to meet people so different from ourselves. We have arrived a few days ago on the island of Te Pito O te Henua[tt], more commonly known as "Easter Island". It is the most isolated inhabited island in the world, four thousand kilometres from any other inhabited place. I had travelled this strange island from one end to the other, a long time ago, it was in 1983, during a speleo-ethnographic mission that I orchestrated. I then forged strong links with a few pascuans, explored caves in which I had made exciting discoveries useful for understanding their history[uu]. Leaving this island had been almost impossible, but this time I'm going back with good company. This island is unique in its history, culture ... it's like an other world.

At the foot of Rano Raraku, the moaï[14] quarry, we met Emma, the niece of one of my former sculptor friends. She then slipped me a question that was close to her heart, she wanted to know if, during my first expedition, her uncle Juan had taken me to visit the family's taboo site, I immediately reassured her. During my readings of exploration stories transmitted by Western navigators who had landed on the island since 1722, I had detected between the lines the existence of these consecrated and very well hidden places, I had

---

[tt] "Te pito o te henua" means: The navel of the world, the island was later named by the discoverer Jacob Roogeven "Easter Island" because discovered on Easter 1722. J. Cook visited the island in 1774 and La Pérouse in 1786.

[uu] The Ana Mata Ki Te Rangi cave ("the cave from which stars are observed") near the ahu Tahai was an initiation cave (as were many others), the entrance porch located between the world of light and the world of darkness served as a place of observation and learning about the constellations. I spotted two basins near the porch dug into the stone, which were filled with water and used as a mirror to indirectly observe the stars.

perceived the rituals practiced and the layout of these sacred sites, but out of respect for this people, I always refused, despite some invitations, to break the taboo of these places.

Yesterday, we buried the scallop deeply in a place that we felt magical and connected, so strong because of its past ! The setting up was, you can imagine, quite supernatural and moving, the connection is now created.

Doc Faust : The unfailing bond you have forged with the scallop will be there to remind you every day of what has happened here.

Mikaël : I drew a circle in the sand, meditated for a few moments and communicated with the elders' spirit.

Doc Faust : You must have had some great moments !

Mikaël : Yes, the hardest part is that it is difficult to realize the importance of the moment, the ritual, the place,... Well, that's what I fell now. It was too strong for a little man, a bit like being crushed by this singular adventure !

Doc Faust : I've never been to Easter Island, but isn't it a crossroads in connection with alchemy ?

Mikaël : This island is, like any place, an alchemical site. We must be in the moment but with a feeling of reliving the emotion of the past. Thus, for example, I explored the caves of Motui nui; this islet located one kilometre from the island has been, since the 18th century, the scene of a strange quest : the quest of the first egg laid. To end the clan wars, the tribal chiefs agreed to elect as spiritual leader and representative of the god Make Make on the island the one whose servant would bring back from the islet, after a long wait in the cave, the first egg of the year. The cult of the Tangata manu (Man - bird) was thus instituted. The Tangata manu elected for a year became "taboo" and withdrew from the secular world. The volatile was thus fixed, and fixed it vanished...

We listen, we observe, we feel, it is intense to be in harmony and thus merge with nature. Man is a grain of sand in front of this immensity. The conjunction is done or not ! So it was one evening, waiting for the sun to set by the ocean, very close to a statue - moai called the Ko Te Riku placed on the ahu Tahai. Pernelle then saw the evolution, all around it, like a blue and white aura. She perceived the energy emanating from the island through this moai, and a tangible link was established between them. It was a magical moment. It was his front door !

The return to reality kept a perfume of strangeness. Omnipresent, strong and contrasting fragrances. Well maybe because you find there a pleasant and sweet smell of laterite, eucalyptus and ocean, an animal smell of wild horses...

Doc Faust *:* The perception of odours awakens a true alliance here and now ! During miracles, some holy places exhaled strong smells of rose. Time is a perverse master where the future is combined with the past in your present.

Mikaël *:* A complete symbiosis, without the imprint of time. Before, when we travelled, we always took a little soil or sand with us from the areas we visited. This ritual gesture is always a way to give sacred meaning to this intuitive relationship.

Alchemical introduction through the middle way

Doc Faust : When you deposit an object with recollection the link is created, but once back... will it be memories or will you really be able to maintain it ? Your dispossession is a form of archetype that concentrates your will and thoughts into a form and a link between two points in space. An interesting experiment, if the link within space is made between you, your matter and the universe, then it would be interesting to renew the experience not in space but in time.

Mikaël : It is not easy to say or demonstrate, it is subjective, we are in the field of perception and sensation. For me, the connection with the heart and soul is very real. Like the quantum relationship between the two parts of the same fragmented object. It is up to us to try to bring this relationship to life, to demonstrate it, to repeat it !

Doc Faust : It's a theory hard to verify. In any case, it is a real work that you have launched, an anchoring of two archetypes that will communicate with each other. It's a bit like taking two cans, drilling a hole in the bottom of each one, and then connecting them with a stretched wire. The oscillation of the wire will convey the message between the transmitter and the receiver. It is the ancestor of the telephone, or even more, the relationship of a wave between two bodies. In our case you have two cans in two different places and a link that doesn't attach to any thread.

Mickaël : The scallop is divided into two parts more than fifteen thousand kilometres apart, the magic path is now traced and the two places are honoured and connected. The druids did this : they took a part of where they came from to where they were to find their destiny. Also, the Polynesians, leaving to colonize a distant land, took a sacred stone from their *marae-altar*, they took it with them to the new island to make it the germ of their new *marae*, so all the islands were connected. It seems that this symbolism is universal !

It is the scallop who commands now, we are spectators of her action, she is the manifestation of the message that passes from one reality to another

Doc Faust : And in addition, you use it as a vehicle of communication as the Spirit does by conveying messages from the Body to the Soul, and from the Soul to the Body !

The main thing is the representation that everyone makes of the moment, as well as they approach the truth. Anchors are guides, no matter what their meaning in the world, as long as they speak to you.

What you do with your shells, the alchemist does with his matter and the heavens.

The priority is to avoid getting lost as much as possible, not to waste too much time, get to the essentials on your journey. We must not tie ourselves up in the useless.

Mikaël : All this raises questions, it's so much on the margins of our current science.

Doc Faust : Truth is a work that is constantly being put back on the loom.

Mikaël : I do indeed ask myself this kind of question regularly, where does the man come from ? Where is it located ? Where is he going ?

Alchemical introduction through the middle way

Doc Faust : The man who wonders is a man who can be touched by grace !

As in the film "2001, the odyssey of space"[vv], before the monolith they were monkeys, then they struck stones to make tools...

Mikaël : Then menhirs, pyramids, statues... and the moai of Easter Island !

Doc Faust : A monument that rises to heaven : Moai, monolith, menhir, needle,... like the vowel I channel of the spirit that descends to earth. Or also, the vertical line in the cross represents the spirit inscribed in the transversal, itself a representation of the horizon of matter.

Behind the words of the birds' language, there are also letters like the electre, the Y for the rebis, the double thing or double spirit, the two lights of the alchemists who come together in one thing. The X is the fire from above and the fire from below, the crucible cross where the spirit descended to a point in the matter.

Mikaël : What you say makes me think of the menhir (high stone) as opposed to the dolmen (stone table). The high stone rises to the sky. It is a link between the bottom and the top, like the common phallic representations, like the statues of Easter Island. Indeed, the moai represent the divinized ancestors, messengers linking the living to the gods. Also, in 1978, our friend Sergio, archaeologist, discovered

---

[vv] « 2001, l'Odyssée de l'espace » film de Stanley Kubrick réalisé en 1968 / "2001, The Space Odyssey" film by Stanley Kubrick directed in 1968

during excavations that the statues carried white coral eyes and an iris of red lava or black obsidian to give them life.

On the other hand, the horizontal dolmen serves as a cave-tomb where darkness recalls the original cave-refuge, the mother's womb; it is a return to the matrix, a return to the raw material.

Doc Faust *:* For menhirs, whether they are carved like in Filitosa or on Easter Island, it doesn't matter, they are needles, vortexes that go from earth to heaven. Like acupuncture in humans, they are used to discharge the earth's overflowing energy or to channel it. This method is found in some cathedrals with the touchstone or discharge stone of the companions. For dolmens, they are like capacitors, amplifiers from earth to earth. There was a time when patients were placed under the table to be treated with the energy of the ground.

Mikaël *:* We are back on our journey from island to island, with beautiful encounters and exchanges, very serene, unlike the dizzying Western world. Here, every word is important, so many right and wise words !

Maori live in the present moment, imbued with their rich ancestral culture. Thus, in front of them, we find our human dimension, without artifice. My spiritual approach here takes on its full meaning. In the West we have to produce every day to exist, whereas here we are in the continuity of the moment before, without generational break.

Doc Faust *:* The more you are in touch with people close to nature and its origins, the better the "mana", the supernatural power that a person or a group possesses. So the mind can fill you if you have emptied yourself well. You will progress more during this trip than

Alchemical introduction through the middle way

in several years with your compatriots in France. But for you, the movement had begun and you have left with the void in you to fill.

Mikaël : Before I left, I suspected that this trip would be intense. But now, despite my knowledge of this part of the world, the shock is stronger than during my two previous trips here ! With each previous return, I had trouble resynchronizing myself physically to our world. This time, I don't think I've lost my palpable landmarks, and that's not important in fact, but the fundamentals are shaken. It will make a deeper upheaval in me, a real alchemical work of dissolution...to rebuild me differently...

Doc Faust : Always live what you receive on a daily basis. The way this is done is up to you. Either you keep everything in you, or you diffuse, you transmit... your mode of participation and restitution to the world is up to you, according to the moment, to your desire, or to what is in front of you.

Mikaël : It is difficult to imagine for the moment how this will be done. To transmit, yes certainly... but only a view of the mind because it is difficult to convey things from the realm of feeling, those experienced intimately. To pass it on, you don't have to write or talk, but create situations where you can make people feel. Many details will come up in due course. It is not mentalized, the heart will speak.

Doc Faust : You are not aware yet of everything you have experienced, do not plan in advance, be attentive to what is happening, your experience makes you more sensitive than before, so be even more attentive. The signs will appear to help you, because

Alchemical introduction through the middle way

it is not you who totally decides but a higher consciousness that shows you the way, even if you are part of the experience.

Mikaël : Staying awake, trusting your instinct, trusting your destiny, this is the quest....

Doc Faust : Alchemy is a Mount Everest, so it is a long-term task.

Mikaël : This is how I imagine the conquest, as when younger during my difficult incursions into the abyss. Especially those of the Pierre Saint Martin and the Gouffre Berger, or with Pernelle and our young son in the high mountains, we had to put our feet in the right place, in the stone and snow, because each act was vital. We always went higher to approach the immensity of the sky and taste the silence in stillness. Risking your life, isn't that starting to live it ? To accept physical and moral suffering is to give a tangible dimension to life. It is through physical effort that we take care of our bodies, and then we can enjoy life ! When the summit is reached, suffering instantly gives way to ecstasy and contemplation.

Doc Faust : The mountaineer will never conquer a mountain, but by making an ascent he achieves the conquest of himself.

Mikaël : The path of life is an Everest to climb, you have the choice to climb it or stay down, stay on the path, climb a part and go down again.

Doc Faust : The Westerner in search of spirituality needs an external material support to charge, he seeks his raw material (*prima materia*). Working on the *prima materia* helps to find a mediator, a mirror in which to be reflected.

He needs to visualize because he is in the material, he externalizes before receiving again. In Asia, man works directly on himself, he internalizes and does not need an execution support that would send him back his reflection

Mikaël : In Polynesia, people not only use their mouths but also their eyes and sometimes their gestures to make money. The Westerner has closed himself on his mouth and his mind, he has restricted his ability to communicate and therefore to rise.

Doc Faust : I would say that man is both transmitter and receiver of his five senses (six senses for the initiate), the spiritual man is the sum of his senses, which could mean that the radiation sent or received during illumination is an added meaning. As with the death of the Egyptian pharaohs, the ultimate and sacred act of closing the mouth was performed. After the verb, the last breath.

Mikaël : The simple man is spontaneous and does not ask himself unnecessary questions, the Western man wants to understand everything, to frame everything, to name everything and, as a result, loses himself in wanting to individualize everything.

Doc Faust : This point is fundamental, and it is from these differences in conception and perception that we can make a good or bad initiation start.

Mikaël : The sixth sense is the one we seek in vain while it is within us.

Doc Faust : The sixth sense is activated long before the philosopher's stone is absorbed, it is accentuated throughout the journey. But for a possible absorption, are we really talking about swallowing Christ as a whole ? Humility would have it to be only his immaculate part.

Mikaël *:* Before this last trip, I had never felt the expression in the looks so much. It penetrated me deep inside myself. A face turned only for a moment towards me and then, instantly, a communion, created by a kind of extrasensoriality, invades us.

Doc Faust *:* A bit like the light of our philosophy, we find it manifested, but we know neither its origin nor its composition. We don't know anything, but it's there. By merging, the philosopher radiates with his whole body like a manifested aura, super luminous, visible by others awake ones. But let's remain modest with all this. Two people in contact are connected even if an infinite distance away. How to find words that describe a modified state of consciousness. For your consciousness is transmuted, the test of time helps you to realize it. These awakings are called singularities, signs...

Mikaël *:* That's right, I'm approaching this state of consciousness, because before, the more I progressed, the more I had the feeling that the "sky" was moving away. Now that I am calm, I can see my progress better on the way : signs, connections and synchronisms are flowing in, but I take care to not wake up my ego. The right balance allows you to situate yourself properly with others but we should be careful not to have too high self-esteem in exchanges and sharing.

Doc Faust *:* It is very complicated both to remain humble, and to leave your own judgment to the person you are accompanying. Talking is already influencing. So to maintain free will, speaking will be done by allegories in order to give a vision and not our vision.

Alchemical introduction through the middle way

One can only convince himself, the Holy Spirit cannot penetrate by force, but by recognizing the light that exists in the other.

Without recognition of light, the student will reject the word of the enlightened. Since the state of evolution is not the same between the two protagonists, only the light of the Holy Spirit can reconcile them. There was a time when transmitting was like proselytizing : by trying too hard and doing too much, we often get nothing. As goes the saying : jack of all trades, master of none... The truth is the truth, but the apprehension of it differs according to your state of receptivity and according to your own progress.

It is simply his experience of overcoming trials that transforms him into a material ready to receive the sacred fire.

Mikaël : That's what I admired from the Polynesians : the frank word, the truth in the moment, the sobriety, the humility.

Doc Faust : The speech is always the same, why do you choose one person over others ? No idea, it is done with some and not with others. It is a question of mutual openness, context, receptivity, empathy... We are the chosen one on our way ! It is in the footsteps of nature that you have to slip your own.

Mikaël : Yes, no rush to find out. Work on your material in nature because it is the largest of the laboratories we have at our disposal. Gnosis must be a sequence and not a beginning. Know little but know well.

Doc Faust : Multiple readings lose the beginner. A few well-chosen books are enough for learning. "Burn the books" said the philosopher, it's on purpose ! Working in the laboratory is also a form of meditation on the aim of our quest.

We set out on a path when we imagine the goal to be achieved. Knowing your goal no longer requires any books, but experimentation in the laboratory is like a bridge to its realization. Here are some authors whom I recognize as true philosophers by fire.

Take note of these, you don't need much : Altus, Artephius, Cosmopolite, Henri Coton-Alvart, Cyliani, Jean d'Espagnet, Nicolas Flamel, Fulcanelli, Raymond Lulle, Philalèthe, Pontanus, Limojon de Saint Didier, Sabine Stuart de Chevalier, Synesius, The baron of Tschoudy, Basile Valentin... But I will think about giving you a chronological list to read and study... However, reading alone is not enough, you must respect the right balance between *Ore* and *Labore*!

Back to the laboratory

A very strange feeling after such a long absence…

"But if we want to make the Art, we must first possess Science, secondly know the goal we desire, thirdly have in us the desire to achieve it, which is the Word"- The genesis of Azoth, Henri Coton-Alvart.

Alchemical introduction through the middle way

Mikaël : About that, I worked yesterday in the laboratory. It's the first time since we got back. I brought the scallop under the oratory into tune with the one on Easter Island. I merged the soil from the island with the one from here. To finalize the connection, I took two drops of alkaest and emptied out myself.

Last night, I was awakened by a strange dream : I had the feeling of having like a ball of love that sprang from my heart, it swelled slowly until it spread around me in the room. A very curious and wonderful feeling. It had nothing to do with the feeling I felt a few years ago, during an N.D.E. (near-death experience) or perhaps an astral exit, it was then a climb into a tunnel of incredibly white and indescribable light, an elevation in serenity and Love. Love enveloped me while this time it exhaled directly from me ! I was receiving it then... Now, I'm transmitting it.

Doc Faust : The alkaest is a connector to the universe in which you live and an amplifier of who you are. Don't forget that it's a hen with golden eggs, it's a huge gift, be its guardian and don't forget what happened in the tale. The message written in your alkaest is actually from you, the guardian of its flame. One day you will be able to split it in two and if it is in line with tradition, offer it to one of your follower.

Mikaël : I am well aware of this, the new encounters of the last few months, everything I have experienced... It is a bliss and a privilege to experience all this. It will have to be left to the right person. It is also a test of faith to find it.

Doc Faust : We are allowed to believe that all this is not related, but my experience makes me affirm that we form a connected whole where each impact on a point on the canvas has an impact on the rest of the canvas !... and the center of the canvas where the vibrations are strongest is like the cenacle that we form.

Mikaël : It's incredible to conceive, I think everything is linked, I'm the actor, but also to a lesser degree the scriptwriter !

Doc Faust : Modified states of consciousness are difficult to identify, analyze and quantify. It will therefore be the accumulation of witnesses that will confirm that all this is not by chance, but rather the same effects that are repeated over and over again.

It is in this state of mind that we could treat terminally ill people who would only have a few weeks to live. The goal would not be to thwart their destiny, just to give them time to organize themselves here on earth. So prudence and humility, we do not oppose official medicine and we do not know the negative effects of alkaest. Caution... We are just men and under no circumstances the equals of our creator.

In the laboratory, alchemy is monitored like milk on the fire, it is a warning, because the unworthy puffer would see the light blind it instead of illuminating it. Sometimes it takes time, but the sanction is inevitable.

Mikaël : Of course, it takes time to reflect, to choose, to decide and then to act, even if I still lack practice, I am making great progress.

Doc Faust : There is a time for everything. A moment of introspection, like a moment of stillness, this intermediate state between being and not being can allow you to receive grace. There is no point in going to church every day if you don't know how to create the intensity of the moment. Without the work of the mind on matter, there is no light. It says, "Knock and we'll open it for you, ask and you'll receive."[ww] but it was never said that you shouldn't make an effort to receive.

Getting in sync and aligning yourself with the real word is a prerequisite. If the true word slips over you like rain drips on the leaf, you won't be able to go very far on the way and you will go in circles.

Mikaël : Indeed, be careful not to adhere to collective schemes that are only simulacrum of path and purpose. It is the endless misguidedness in the maze.

Doc Faust : Everyone determines his own path, practice is only a tool to pass through the doors faster, but the path is in you, the road : it's you ! The destination is where your mind can lead you. If you don't understand what it means to destroy the ego, then you get caught up in the veil of appearances and lose all sense of reality.

The best I can wish you is at some point to take the road alone. You will then move from apprentice to companion.

Mikaël : Yes, even if accompanied, I know that I am alone on the way, if you think otherwise you add a veil instead of removing it. It's like in Chartres where we go through the labyrinth every year.

[ww] Gospel according to St. Matthew 7-7: "Ask, and it will be given to you; seek, and you will find; knock, and it will be opened to you".

Alchemical introduction through the middle way

You sit in front of the entrance, remove your metals and shoes, walk it barefoot, alone in a deep state of meditation where nothing weighs on you, no object or question. The labyrinth is made of black and white stones. The number of white stones to be covered is not the result of chance, the length in cubits of the path to be covered represents nine months, the duration to pass from darkness to light, everything is symbolically inscribed here to represent a long life of quest to find its center.

Doc Faust : Some people think they are on the road when they have not yet packed their bags.

Mikaël : This is the difference between a saturated bag and a properly filled bag, on an expedition the overfilled bag will not take you very far, even if you feel you have done it well. The first step would be to unpack the bag and replace only a few essential items. A well-prepared bag will help you travel well. In life it's the same, we take a lot of useless things and appear, but we will leave as we came. It is only a question of leaving our testimony to history, not to be part of history. We are and will remain anonymous on the way, that's why we only sign our books with our pseudonyms. We are nothing and we will do everything to stay that way.

Doc Faust : If the student wants to hand in his non essence-cial stuff, he will stay at the entrance and be blocked at the first door. It is identical for alchemy in the laboratory, we work on a support, a stone to cut, it becomes the mirror of oneself, it is an introspection that allows us to understand ourselves without lying about our evolution. For if you lie to your stone, you lie to yourself.

Alchemical introduction through the middle way

Mikaël : Knowing how to organize your bag for the expedition on the way, constantly questioning yourself, agreeing to purge the superfluous to welcome the spark.

Doc Faust : Once the journey begins, we unconsciously ask questions to the path and receive the answers from heaven... But it is the penitent who will transform the answers into experiences or, more paradoxically, the answers into new questions. I think the practice of energy care has helped you to receive this spark.

Mikaël : The question is always more important than the answer !

Doc Faust : The question is the answer ! To move from question to answer, you have to work. The inspiring one gives you direction, but does not lead you by the hand on the way. To G-et OLD without B-ury, you must E-laborate !

Mikaël : Giving an answer without getting to the core of the problem does not help, especially if a new question arises every time...

Doc Faust : The work of an initiate is to put gold in oneself, to make the light from above meet the spark from below. Henri Coton-Alvart referred to the work as the reunification of the two lights.

On the other hand, taking the middle way has some danger. In the laboratory, even if one must not think like a chemist, the chemist's safety rules are essential... A blacksmith without his ceremonial mask could not, in the fumes, be a perfect little alchemist for very long.

Mikaël : The professions related to metalworking are noble ! They are often a component of the mastery required for some laboratory work. For me, the last few years have been great, so in continuity, the following ones give hope...

Doc Faust : Do you see yourself forging in your garden and playing Hephaestus with metals against each other ?

Mikaël : Everything seems possible to me. I will have to go in search of tools, build an oven, master the Art of Fire, find the materials.

Doc Faust : The first rule is : fumes are toxic to you and nature, so it is essential to find a way to avoid polluting you and others. Always work with respect for what surrounds you to elevate yourself. You will have to get into shape... For the basic technical side, I recommend reading Jean Laplace's "*Rudimentum Alchimiae*". This writing is a continuation of the works : "*The alchemy on its classical writtings*" by Eugène Canseliet, "*The Alchemical Laboratory*" by Atorène or "*The Alchemical Golden book*" by Jean-Pascal Percheron.

But beware these regulus' colors have never approached a hint of the alchemical truth, they just gave some interesting experiences for our work.

You're committing to years of ungrateful work. The first metallurgical work, and not alchemical, I insist... is to find at the forge the *regulus* (little king), you will have to melt a hundred times your material before mastering the art of fire, purify your materials, lower the melting temperatures with fluxes. This is what the puffers of the past and modern times do, but every worker must start there.

Nowadays, doing this work is a bit like getting up at dawn to pick the dew from the fields. It is a ritual, a tradition, a folklore that makes you feel the magic of the road. Melting a regulus is part of it even if it complicates the understanding of the work to be done, look at the book "*The alchemical Labora-T-ore*". There is a nice warning in this story.

I grant you that knowing the Way of Santiago, we want to continue it. We then head towards Fisterra, dreaming of finding a few starry nodules, to see that with his knowledge at the end of the road, we will have travelled the earth. Like Nicolas Flamel on his return from Compostela, we will then have to think about returning home by the sea, because like any true philosopher, we will have to make the dry follow by the wet.

Afterwards, you will seek light in the seven metals, you will make the sacred lamp of the temple of Abydos shine, you will make the glass that stops part of the sunlight, you will grow in your philosophical garden the most remarkable gems and you will heal the most needy. But above all, you will come into contact with your creator and you will form an ark of covenant by doing, when the aura of light covers you down here, with what is above, what is below.

But let's go back to the first door. There are symbolically twelve of them, but there are actually many more to invent and new shortcuts or detours to find. For days, whether it is snowing, windy or raining, you will work this hell paved with good intentions until it becomes the most beautiful philosophical garden.

Mikaël : We are looking to develop our equipment... Looking for ways to do better at each melt, understand each phase and where it is wrong. If we do the operation again using the same way, it is useless. But is it only at the forge that we are on the middle way ?

Alchemical introduction through the middle way

Doc Faust : We complicate, we use cunning, we want precision, but the work of nature is so simple that a single fire is enough to perfect the work. The middle way doesn't need the forge, it's true.

The material must communicate with you, and you with it, but at first it doesn't want to, so you must defeat the dragon, under no circumstances pierce the one in your womb, but strike down the guardian of the material... put it in the ground, so that the material opens, so that the demon opens his mouth and spits out his flames. To do this, you will use the sword and shield. As staged in the Saint Michael fountain in Paris, you will harass the demon and put a bit on him to channel it to your will, until he gives in and finally the two fires can find each other.

May the fire from below meet the fire from above, so that life may be given to matter and the miracle of resurrection may be repeated again.

Mikaël : I have a real communication with nature, trees and stones, but I didn't think I would be communicating with metal any time soon. I know that he is alive and that the discussion with him must not be easy.

Doc Faust : There is no such thing as metal. The metallic universe interests us only for its shape, its crystalline mesh, and it is much closer than you think to your mineral water.

Mikaël : Now you're talking to my geologist and speleologist heart !

Doc Faust : When a matter receives the spirit (fire, the grace of God), it takes on a capital letter and thus the raw material becomes the source material. Likewise, the adept becomes an Adept if he has been able to keep the spirit without perverting it.

Mikaël : Crystallized light ?

Doc Faust : No, the light fixed in a crystal, which is not the same. As René Louis Vallée[xx] would say in his book "La synergétique", it is a collapse of the electron barrier, the K capture.

Because what is fixed can be volatilized and left : Light to Matter and Matter to Light... The Matter becomes transparent and receives the original light that is then manifested.

Matter is composed, according the the alchemical conceptions, of a soul for a third (sulfur), to which are added a third of body (salt), and a third of spirit (mercury). Anything that would be added would be faeces and filth and would disrupt the order of things.

Mikaël : Matter is thus the Whole, like the Ouroboros, the snake represented in a loop ?

Doc Faust : Yes, with a capital letter, Whole ! Like Thut - Universe (Egyptian god) that is symbolized by an arch, like the Celtic dolmen. In ancient Egypt, $Tho(u)t^{yy}$, is the first month of the Nilotic calendar

---

[xx] « L'énergie électromagnétique matérielle et gravitationnelle- Hypothèse d'existence des milieux énergétiques et d'une valeur limite supérieure du champ électrique » éditions Masson 1971 / "Material and gravitational electromagnetic energy - Hypothesis of the existence of energetic environments and an upper limit value of the electric field " Masson éditions ; 1971.
[yy] T(h)out as "tout" in French which means all

Alchemical introduction through the middle way

based on the Nile flood, which corresponds to July and August in our country.

Thut[*] - Thot, becomes like Thau, hence a certain palace of the Tau in Reims. As you will have noticed in Flamel, the Tau is another form of the caduceus

If you observe the caduceus, the two snakes form the Alpha and the top of the caduceus, the inverted wings, the Omega. Wouldn't the alpha be the "heli-colloidal" form of DNA, the original message we are looking for ?

Thus, we find on the sceptre of the Adept, in the order of operation, the crossing of the elements four times... I would not say more but whoever knows will understand why I hold in high esteem the names of Solomon, James and Soubise.

When you move around in a church, on candles you will find the same Alpha and Omega. Hermes the messenger who travels between heaven and earth. Its attributes are in its caduceus, and if you go from alpha to omega, you turn it upside down by making One the Whole. The mind stares at the volatile and volatilizes the fixed.

On the caduceus, fixed snakes become volatile and volatile wings become fixed.

---

[*] In French, Whole = Tout (TN)

Alchemical introduction through the middle way

To move from the One to the Whole, there will be seven allegorical days, seven bars on scale, seven days at creation. It reminds me of the first alchemical writing that we slipped into the genesis :

"In the beginning, God created the heavens and the earth. The earth was formless and empty : there was darkness on the surface of the abyss, and the spirit of God moved above the waters."[zz]

Mikaël : Seven... That's Four Elements and Three Principles !

As on the Tetraktys we saw before : Water, Earth, Air, Fire become three principles : Sulfur, Salt and Mercury principles, which in turn

---

[zz] Bible: Genesis 1, The Origins of the World and Humanity, the first account of creation.

Alchemical introduction through the middle way

become Sulfur and Mercury of the philosophers, who through the consecrated marriage will form the Chrysopoeia !

Four plus three equals seven, plus two equals nine, the scale of philosophers, plus one gives the chrysopheus.

Is there a connection with the sculpture of Cybele depicted with a nine-bar ladder on the porch of Notre Dame de Paris ?

Doc Faust : Yes, as MICHAIEL is the anagram of ALCHIMIE[*], Cybèle, symbol of Nature is only one more symbol to tell us that it is alchemy. We find Cybèle under other names : "Mother of the gods or Great Goddess".

It is the symbol of the wild power of nature. She is also the divinity of fertility. Look at this symbol now : Chi (Tau), Rhô (X), and Alpha and Omega.

---

[*] Alchimie = alchemy in french (TN).

Alchemical introduction through the middle way

The Christian symbol is in fact a representation of Hermes. Again, isn't it strange, this labyrinth of Chartres with a minotaur or Tau-Rhô[*] in its centre, recipient of sunlight and elementary symbol of fire ? The minotaur with the body of a man and the head of a bull is the son of Pasiphae and a white bull. He will be locked by Minos in the labyrinth.

---

[*] Phonetically Tau-Rhô is as Taureau, wich means bull, in French. TN

The morning dew

The morning dew
In the best days of spring, the Adepts would get up before sunrise and start harvesting dew by hitting the plants with a stick. This dew was collected in a glass dish and filtered...
Élixir de longue vie et la Pierre philosophale de Rumélius - A. Barbault 1948 (Long life elixir and the philosopher's Stone by Rumélius – A. Barbault, 1948).

Hermes at Bilbao

"On the false road of spring
is the dew of the fields,
While at the top of our balloon
takes place the one and only sublimation.

This true celestial water
is our mercury rising and falling off after,
because only the spirits vanished into thin air
act and fix our matter

All of you, sons of Hermes, be assured.
"That I don't want you to be injured.
But without further detour with my saying.
You're a thousand miles away from the thing.

For if celestial dew to the gods what is above is.
For men, we need the water that the sea gives.
So don't work only in the spring.
But all year long be in the lab working !"

Doc Faust

Alchemical introduction through the middle way

Mikaël : What is above is like what is below... The whole work works by analogy, so can we do without the celestial dew down here ?

Doc Faust : What is in heaven is reserved for God, the dew is part of it, what is on earth is reserved for men and that is enough. Since the gods do not mix with men, celestial dew is not the dew that we will use in our balloon.

Mikaël : It's true that we have everything here, it's quite right !

Doc Faust : "What's up is like what's down" but it's never been said that you have to mix up with down.

Mikaël : But when you say "the water of the sea", is it practical or is it an allegory ?

Doc Faust : The water of the bitter[*]... has a strong relationship with the vitriol, the Vitri-oleum, the truth that comes out of the well. "*Visita Interiora Terrae Rectificandoque Invenies Occultum Lapidem*" or "Visit the interior of the earth, and by correcting yourself will find the hidden stone".

---

[*] *Bitter* in french is « *L'amer* » and sounds like "*La mer*" = *the sea* (TN).

Alchemical introduction through the middle way

V.I.T.R.I.O.L.

More truths for the lost seeker. You shouldn't have learned... "Happy the simple-minded", a happy man in fact ! A fertile field where it is easy to sow. Nature is not complicated. Why should the work be different ?

Mikaël : And we often complicate the way ! You have to be sane, and intuitive.

Doc Faust : Few alchemists understand all this, many will always remain to vegetate. On your side, if you can make a way of life out of what you learn, you will move forward. So when we teach and share, we learn more from others than they learn from you. As you evolve, you must not forget where you come from. Your duty is to lighten your neighbour in the present so that he can chart his path in the future

Mikaël : We are above all the student's student, we learn from him.

Doc Faust : This is quite similar to what happened with Saint Christopher[15]. One day, the Christ appeared as a young boy who wanted to cross a river. For a man the size of Christopher, it seemed it would be easy to put this boy on his shoulders and walk into the water. Yet, as soon as he had begun the crossing, the water began to rise and his burden became heavier and heavier, to such an extent that he had to support himself on his stick. Bravely, Christopher continued his crossing, but the water was still rising and the child's weight was weighing him down again and again; the giant thought he was about to die in these raging waves. But in a last effort, he tore himself from the waves with his burden and reached the shore safely.

"The Colossus of Saint Christopher of Notre Dame de Paris"

Alchemical introduction through the middle way

It was then that the child revealed his identity, he was Jesus Christ, the "Light of the world", so the giant did not carry a simple child, but the world as a whole. In front of the unbelieving smuggler, the child asked him to plant his stick in the ground, near his house and go to rest. The next day when Christopher woke up, he found the stick covered with leaves and fruit. He knew then that he had carried the light of the world and took the name of light carrier "Christ-ophorus" which by simplification gave "Offerus".

In another way, we could say that light, which is the Full, presses on the matter which is empty. Thus, the cruciferous globe represents the matter inscribed in the tetramorph : Water, Earth, Fire, Air.

Mikaël : Once again we find the basis of the Tetraktys with the four elements, the four cardinal virtues, the three principles and the three theological virtues. Moreover, isn't the stick of Saint Christopher similar to the spear of Saint George terracing the dragon ? As well as to the valiant sword of Saint Michael[aaa] ?

Doc Faust : Nature repeats itself and so do allegories. On the representation of the Tetraktys, replaces the term "principle" with "sages" or "philosophers", then "silver" with "Mercury" and "gold" with "sulphur". You will then have the alchemical process of transforming chaos into light, the Archangel Saint Michael being only the fire that gives life to the dead matter. The whole philosophy is there !

[aaa] De l'hébreu Mîkhâ'êl ou en latin « Quis ut Deus » soit « Qui est égal à Dieu », le messager de Dieu. / From the Hebrew Mîkhâ'êl or in Latin "Quis ut Deus" or "Who is equal to God", the messenger of God.

Alchemical introduction through the middle way

In heaven, it is God's gift "*Donum Dei*". But on earth, let's talk a little bit about the self-giving "*Donum Intuiti*". It is a kind of counter-power to what is being done everywhere because so-called holders of hermetic science violate our traditional teachings for trade and glory. So it is a bit like an evangelist's mission to spread the good word, the true word for which our savior climbed on the cross.

You should write a book to record your questions and thoughts, to synthesize all our words. It would be useful to some people including yourself. This writing exercise helps to organize thoughts when it is very difficult in conversations to establish a chronology.

Mikaël : I accept this mission, with joy and humbleness. It will be a new door to be opened. Above all, I will have to remain faithful to the spirit of the Great Art that you are trying to teach me. All our exchanges have been saved, and I will do my best to record them as soon as we return from our trip.

Pilgrimage to Santiago de Compostela

Every morning we take the road, every morning we go further. Day after day and again tomorrow. Ultreïa ! Ultreïa ! E sus eia Deus adjuva nos ! The way of earth and the way of faith...

For some time now, an idea was making its way, Mikaël wanted to undertake this pilgrimage, he had been dreaming of it for a long time. To visit this inner path, you had to be ready and present, it seemed that this moment had finally arrived...

Alchemical introduction through the middle way

Mikaël : It is said that you have to live, once in a lifetime, a part of the way to Santiago de Compostela. We're not young anymore, but doing it by walking or by any other means doesn't really matter. A friend told me that he had made another shell path, from the north of France to Mount Saint Michel, under the most extreme conditions. There he experienced extraordinary things that only he could tell you. Later, he spent fifteen days in the solitude of a monastery and found that he felt almost the same effects as on the path.

Doc Faust : Each pilgrim follows the path for a reason of his own. No need to be baptized, initiation is above all spiritual. Only the spirit of the path counts, even if walking the "Camino" is an adventure in itself, certainly very physical. We find the idea of the spirit that transcends the material, the spiritual that opens itself to physical effort.

Mikaël : This confirms my idea and reassures me, because Pernelle and I have decided to follow this path in stages. We stopped in Tours, Poitiers and other places. We then stayed in Saint Jean Pied de Port, an essential stopover, it is the meeting point of all the roads coming from the north before passing through Spain via the Roncesvalles pass.

In tourist shops, we are tempted by walking sticks that insiders call bumblebees. But among these piles of wood, which one to choose ? None of them really seduce us...

Doc Faust : You don't choose a bumblebee, it's an object filled with meaning that you give. If you don't receive such a gift, it comes or is adopted, it is up to you to answer its call, open your heart and let go, I am sure there is one waiting for you. The delivery of the bumblebee

Alchemical introduction through the middle way

consecrates the rite of departure to Compostela. The blessing recalls the two physical and spiritual dimensions of this stick. We find the symbol of the cross, the ground is the horizon and the stick that stands up is the spirit. He'll hammer the ground to bring down the beast with every step.

As it is said : "Receive this rod, comfort against the fatigue of walking on your pilgrimage path, so that you may overcome all the traps of the enemy and reach the sanctuary of Santiago quietly and that, when your goal is reached, you may return to us with joy by the grace of God".

Mikaël : Well, the choice of a bumblebee is a commitment. Nothing here corresponds to the spirit of the pilgrimage, nothing very transcendent, only kevlar sticks or tourist sticks, but certainly nothing built in spirit or tradition. In this world of appearance everything is imitation.

Doc Faust : Soon, I will join you directly in Santiago, perhaps with bumblebees in my luggage. I will contact my friend companion sculptor to see if he can help us in this choice.

Mikaël : Then we couldn't have better sticks !

Doc Faust : I spent all Saturday with my sculptor friend, I knew he was a crafstman *companion*[*] with a path based on values that strongly looks like ours. Here are a few words about our talks…

---

[*] See note about "Compagnon du Devoir"

The craftsman and the alchemist

Ophelia

Work realized by our friend Michel who knew how to breathe the spirit into the material with this magnificent siren.

Alchemical introduction through the middle way

Doc Faust : Where does the Companionship come from ?

Michel : It is a series of legends that have been transmitted... I say legends because, since the beginning, transmission and initiation have always been done in this way, orally. This is still done today....

Doc Faust : Long before that, does it means a connection to the construction of Solomon's temple ?

Michel : Yes, in this chiaroscuro of history, we can see that Solomon, wishing to build a temple, called upon the architect Hiram who started the work. Workers feeling aggrieved waited for the architect at different doors in the walls and three times Hiram received blows that caused his death... his clothes and other belongings were attributed to the different lineages... it was Master James and Father Soubise who took up the torch to complete the temple... Then they took the boat to France and on the way, a dispute broke out that separated them... the three duties were created, under the aegis of King Solomon, Master James and Father Soubise...

Doc Faust : This number three again, that accomplishes the work ?

Michel : This idea of trilogy and Corporations crossed France to Sweden, while passing through Germany and England... and there, there was a new split : a group wanted to integrate "the bourgeois" (the one who did not hold the tool) and created Freemasonry... hence our common symbols : square and compass.

Doc Faust : Since the Andersen conventions, I find that Freemasonry has been very inspired by alchemists, I see that it has also took from the Companions.

Michel : Of course, these are shortcuts, many books talk about them but always based on legends...

Doc Faust : For me, the Companions go hand in hand with the initiates who built the Cathedrals.

Michel : Well, the oldest trace of the Compagnonnage is on the stained glass windows of the Cathedral of Chartres : we can see Workers wearing the flowered ribbon (the Colour) on their forehead, it is around the year 1250. Another record dating from 1480 is on a manuscript at the National Library

Also, we must not forget the Roman invasion, the corporations, their techniques... and also "those of the local people" who also had a knowledge that surprised Julius Caesar, to such an extent that he mentioned it in his writings... everything made our Companionship.

Doc Faust : When did the Companions become known ?

Michel : It was in the 19th century that the Companionship was revealed to the public through the writings of the Companion Agricol Perdiguier. (It should not be forgotten that this group of free and independent men had always scarred Religion, Kings, Emperors and Presidents).

George Sand, moved by his story, wrote about it. At that time, the Companionship cried out for betrayal, for sacrilege.

Doc Faust : Just because we are known to the public does not mean that we should reveal our secrets, we lose the marvel of initiation.

But I thought about the three separate currents... Wouldn't it be better, to form only one, to be stronger ?

Michel : After umpteen epics, Agricol Perdiguier tried to reunite all the old Duties because the dangers of industrialization and fratricidal fighting were beginning to be felt. He failed but, after his death, the movement was launched and it was in 1889 that the Companion Lucien Blanc - with other Brothers - brought together in one all these old Duties, saying "to each his ideas, but between us we speak neither of religion nor of politics". Thus was born the Companionship Union of *Compagnons du Tour de France des Devoirs Unis*.

Doc Faust : We agree, we use the Pythagorean principle a lot and, like you, we prefer to go towards the light of three becoming one.

Michel : Yes, but later, new dissensions and other Societies were created and today three Companions Unions are officially recognized : the *Fédération Compagnonnique des Métiers du Bâtiment et autres Métiers*, the *Association Ouvrière des Compagnons du Devoir et du Tour de France* and *the Union Compagnonnique des Compagnons du Tour de France des Devoirs Unis*[*].

Doc Faust : The companionship is respected in our society, as the guarantor of the quality of old crafts, of know-how, a little like a

---

[*] *Fédération Compagnonnique des Métiers du Bâtiment et autres Métiers* : Companionship union of the building trade and other trades. *Association Ouvrière des Compagnons du Devoir et du Tour de France* : Laborer association of the Companions of Duty and Tour of France. *Union Compagnonnique des Compagnons du Tour de France des Devoirs Unis* : Companionship Union on the Tour of France by United Duty Companions.

memory stored in your hands for eternity.

Michel : UNESCO has made Compagnonnage part of the Intangible Heritage of Humanity and the French State has recognised our public utility corporation.

Doc Faust : A classic question, how do you become a companion ?

Michel : In broad terms... To be a Companion, the Young "Rabbit" with a Professional degree and a job can knock on our door. He will start by observing and then, he will become a Member and will have courses after his working day : courses in draught, workshop, French and mathematics (of course, everything will depend on the time and the Society...).

If the Young Person's commitment seems sincere to us, he will be asked to present us with a job that will include some difficulties of the profession, he will have to find a Companion Godfather according to the affinities (preferably in his profession... but not necessarily).

Doc Faust : I heard that to be a companion you have to present a masterpiece ?

Michel : For his first passage, the newbie have to present to his Peers, a Piece that proves that he knows how to live by his craft. He will deconstruct his work by the Art of the line, by his work at the bench, his knowledge of archivist and also his behavior. After a constructive criticism, according to the vote, he will be given his first Color : a green ribbon hung on the buttonhole, near the heart and he will be explained our values during his initiation.

Doc Faust : The color green, we find it in the vegetable kingdom, the green nature is the one that is bright, turbulent, acid or oil, called V.I.T.R.I.O.L.U.M. this color is formed of two acids : a yellow and a blue that fuse in this green color that will corrupt our saturnian lead. It is a very long work to penetrate the land of the alchemists and reach the philosopher's stone.

Michel : With us the young student will have many years to work in order to be able to introduce himself again and to acquire the Red Color. As the difficulties grow, many will give up, the time may also make them eager because it takes about 7 years after the professionnal degree.

Doc Faust : Can an accomplished and inspired worker be a Companion ?

Michel : The particularity of the Companion Union is to extend the tradition of the Ancient Duties; when, in certain regions, there were no Companions, we went to see craftsmen or workers. And if one of them was spotted, after an investigation of morality and knowledge, he was offered to come and join us, knowing that, despite his age and knowledge, he would start as a Young person so that he could become part of our Society; not an easy thing for him because he has a background...

Doc Faust : An old man who becomes young again, the two do not have the same life and family obligations !

Michel : Of course, having a wife and children, we will adjust his new life so that everyone can live this transition well. He will also have to be present on the Tour de France and will have to fulfil Companionship obligations. He will again come to us with a Piece with which he will go into Criticism and, if the vote is positive, he will discover after an initiation that he has been received as a Companion. He will then get his Red Color as well as his Cane.

But this story is only an overview...

Doc Faust : What does Duty mean ?

Michel : The word Duty in the society has a connotation of obligation. The word Duty in Companionship has a different meaning : respect and listening to others to shake up our convictions. The duty of transmission, to help and support our Brothers, without expecting anything in return. Not to be enslaved, not to be served, but to serve, it also means a rule of life that we try at best to practice, to put spirituality in technique. It also means... Companion...

This word is quite new, before we said Saint Duty of God, the Duty Bearers, but also Duty of Liberty... but despite all this, the good spirit, the support of his Brothers in his Companion Society was very much alive.

Doc Faust : It seemed to me that the corporations were stringly united within, but that controversy reigned between corporations ?

Michel : That is why I insist on duty "in his Society" because not so long ago between rival Societies, no merci, wars were common. They killed each other one to one or in gangs fights and when the police intervened, they all agreed to fight this authority and then they would resume their battles. There are police reports that tell of all these brawls with canes, rulers, squares and compasses (not to mention tools). To get an idea, you have to refer to the series "Ardéchois Coeur Fidèle" with all its epics that could have existed

Alchemical introduction through the middle way

(the battle of Tournon).

Doc Faust *:* Alchemists also have their rivalries as evidenced by the verbal jousting on forums. But why is it on your field too ?

Michel *:* Why these wars ? Out of revenge between Duties and to have a city to place Companions in the workshops.

But over time, when we noticed that too many men were killed, we moved the fight and gained cities with masterpieces : everyone was locked in a room with the same tools, the same pieces of wood and when one of them said "finished", everything stopped. Impartial people from other backgrounds voted and the winner had the key to the city for his Company for a specific time; "he had done his Duty". (Of course, it wasn't always that easy).

Doc Faust *:* But all these quarrels are now over ?

Michel *:* Today, these fratricidal wars no longer exist, but the word Duty persists with all its variations :

- ✓ Religious processions still exist were the blessing of tools is done but they are also processions that have no religious connotation.

- ✓ The Duty during banquets; after breaking the bread in a ritual gesture, the Rôleur with his Cane will strike the ground three times and ask us to put ourselves in our Duty... and there, everything stops, conversations, the meal and all other activities to put ourselves in Color :... green, red, white, yellow, blue and put ourselves in a solemn state, in a precise and respectful position to the Companions of yesterday, today and tomorrow...

The Duty is most of all about helping and supporting one's brothers;

in the 13th century already, a form of social security existed, just like this Cane.

Doc Faust : The cane is a very strong symbol among alchemists, it is the caduceus of Hermes which represents the spirit descending on earth.

Michel : The cane is the symbol of Hermes in all his understanding. It is there to remind us that we are eternal pilgrims on the path of knowledge, a quest that will be a life...

We have the duty to learn, to improve our work, on the bench, in archival work to create the future (some professions die but others are born) according to our criteria, we must always transform the matter... We therefore have the duty to pass on the trade so that the following ones can also learn life with a Companion's perspective.

We are only perfectible men, we are eternal children who must not stop learning. We must never let go of the Cane....

Doc Faust : You have just told me about Hermes, who is associated with the Egyptian God Thut. He is, for us, the first Adept and I am surprised that a Companion is interested in Alchemy.

Michel : It seems to me that our quests are similar. For me, it is to take another look, another point of view, to be even more universal.

You only grow up with the other and the mind needs an act, otherwise it is useless. Our gaze that contemplates the horizon is reduced because the earth is round, our body paired with our mind has a greater scope... and the mind lives only by the act.

To know techniques that we could adapt to what we are, to seek

Alchemical introduction through the middle way

golden harmony in its proportion and spiritual harmony for our work.

I am thinking of an image where an Alchemist sits on a manure pile, he disturbs those who look at him with dirty eyes, but our ploughman, just like us, knows that the earth feeds on this manure.

Beyond the metaphysical side, under this manure, the "woody" will put oak wood that the acids will knead to accompany us better in our work. By crossing ideas, it's easiest to move forward.

Of course, it only involves me; every Companion has his own approach.

I must try to know beyond the spirit of the image, the spirit of matter because everything is alive. Even a felled tree continues to live. If it becomes wood for everyone... I still consider it as a living being. Although the common language says that wood lives, because under the action of humidity and heat, it deforms, cracks, etc... it's a reduced idea of « life ». As for me its life just continues : it has been impregnated with the place of the earth where it was born and the present moment, its vitality is still there, the properties of the lunation, the sun are always active, the currents of water and telluric are impregnated.

They are assets for the work I have to do, the material enters me and vice versa. All beings communicate with perceptions, they are the same for all : animal, vegetable, mineral; we are one, we learn it all life long.

Dialog, openness to the other in its entirety and the bench are our tools in this quest for universality.

Alchemical introduction through the middle way

Of course, we stumble on the stones but they are pebbles that help us think. The Companions have done and, for some, are still doing initiation walks and if they can't do it, the confinement is also initiatory... after that we can be fullfilled by less, it is respectable.

But the light !

I am an image-sculptor who, like you, loves symbolism, we also find it very much with us : "the hive with the queen surrounded by her workers... our Cayenne* with our Companion Mother surrounded by the Companions in a chain of alliance".

Our Ancients, alchemists and companions, rubbed shoulders, just look at our cathedrals which still transmit to us today technical and philosophical messages more than 800 years later.

It was done yesterday, can we keep these life messages alive ?

It is up to our goodwill to make this transmission our Duty.

And as the song says...
"Companion, Companion, let's see if the earth is round
Companion, Companion go clear the globe.... »

or even...
"Let us stand up, let us walk with frankness that all hearts may join together, for unity on our Colours let us mark this motto : fraternity, fraternity."

---

* Home of the companions (TN).

Alchemical introduction through the middle way

And now my friend, to our work...

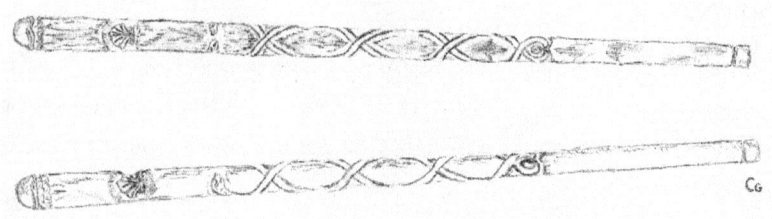

Pilgrim's bumblebees

Doc Faust : ... after this unexpected discussion about companionship along the way, we arrived after turns and detours in the heart of a forest that my friend loves. According to ancient rituals, we went to choose trees. It will be hazelnut tree, a tree used for some rituals as well as for dowser sticks. The particularity of this wood is to be in connection with the energies of the earth. We first asked permission from the chosen branches and explained to them what we planned to dop, tied them up and bled them so that the vital energy would return to the earth.

Then there we prayed in a small chapel set up on a powerful telluric vortex, we cut them at heart height, replanted the upper parts so that they would die in peace, and then peeled the bark.

Once raw, the ritual begins with the one of the air, the earth, and we went to a withdrawn alchemical chapel to present them to the water of a sacred fountain, then finally to the fire.

Alchemical introduction through the middle way

The carefully collected bark was burned and the ashes put back to the ground. The sticks were also blessed three times. They are made in one piece and free of metals, just a protective nail at the foot to avoid wear and tear. But a stick is nothing to us alchemists without our symbolism. Our book both open and closed, we then move on to personalization. Personalization is used to identify the man who holds it, but it must remain sober. We find the impact of the "logos" which in an image summarizes a character, his journey and his level.

For the sculptures, it will be two intertwined snakes, a scallop and an Ouroboros. Four intertwining in the light and three in the dark. The passage from the bare stick to the carved bumblebee is the beginning of the path. This straight and descending "I" like the spirit will make the connection to Santiago where it will again be struck by the four elements : Earth with its path, Water with the horse fountain of Santiago, Air with a short visit of the roofs of the building and Fire with the Botafumeiro inside the cathedral.

Mikaël : How I wished I could be with you then. I had no idea that a pilgrim's cane could be made in this way. We are a far from these tourist sticks seen in the window and sold at a very high price for what they are. They will now be wonderful companions on our path.

Doc Faust : The bumblebees are intended for insiders, otherwise they are desecrated and become dead wood again. It is not a gift but a responsibility, you will have to earn them so that they can carry you.

Mikaël : Yes, we understood it that way. We'll make sure they take us in the right direction. The sticks are very personal and will not be in other hands, that is clear. Just as the blade of a Samurai sword carries the spirit of its ancestors, so a stranger touches it and it's a desecration. For an initiated alchemist, the same applies to his bumblebee.

Doc Faust : Yes, because no one else but you should touch them. The stick is the symbol of the spirit on earth, like the spear of Saint George, only an initiate can approach and "touch" the divine.

The stick you received is yours, now you must desserve it. It will take you a long time to own it. A bumblebee is like a church bell, it resonates with its environment.

The one who presents the stick does so as a sign of allegiance, we are in the same rituals as those of the knights. When you walk with him, you show your respect for the path.

Mikaël : So the stick is like the sword of the knights ?

Doc Faust : Absolutely, it will be very usefull. But don't get me wrong, he's your master. You will have to submit to it, because it actually represents the Holy Spirit...

On the *camino frances* to Santiago

Shrine of the crypt of the cathedral of Santiago de Compostela known to contain the apostle's relics

A few days later in the direction of Santiago de Compostela...

From Saint Jean Pied de Port, the climb is quite steep. The sun is revealed to us through the morning mist... Spain is finally seen. We arrive in Roncesvalles, the atmosphere is hushed, and the enchantment increases as we progress along the road to Santiago.

Alchemical introduction through the middle way

Mikaël : We passed through Spain, at the foot of the pass. The Abbey of Roncesvalles is sober and authentic and... quite austere. An organist tried his hand on the organ... He repeated his scales and each of the notes played vibrated persistently, penetrating us one after the other. The throbbing notes went from the lowest to the highest, taking us ever higher. I was like carried from the darkness to the light.

Now the journey continues on the "Camino Frances"[bbb] with beautiful stops where we discovered so many beautiful Romanesque churches and cathedrals. We crossed Pamplona, Puente la Reina, Estella, the magnificent Burgos, Leon and Sarria before reaching the mythical Santiago de Compostela[ccc] today.

Doc Faust : How do you like Santiago's atmosphere ? For nearly a thousand years, it has been one of the three great pilgrimages of Christianity with Jerusalem and Rome, and it shaped this place.

[bbb] Since the beginning of the 12th century, the Camino Frances has linked Europe and northern Spain. It takes its name from the pilgrims who came to the other side of the Pyrenees and the installation of many Franks along the way. The history of this path has shaped the route and the cities along it. The religious buildings and monuments are a testify of its prestigious past.

[bbb] : *Campus Stellae* (the *star field*) is one of the supposed etymologies for Compostela, referring to the legend that the burial of Santiago was found thanks to a bright star above a Galician field, a field in which the tomb was found.

Alchemical introduction through the middle way

Mikaël : Here, the welcoming of pilgrims by the inhabitants is a tradition. Throughout the city, despite the crowds, there is a serenity mixed with great piety, even for those who are not religious. We first visit the cathedral where we will stay during the week. Going around the building we observed the sculptures and, in the square in front of the north gate, this magnificent three-horse fountain. Like the three principles, they also offer a reminder of the four elements : the webbed hooves for water, the legs for earth, fire by breath and movement, not to mention, of course, by raising one's head, a female divinity in heaven.

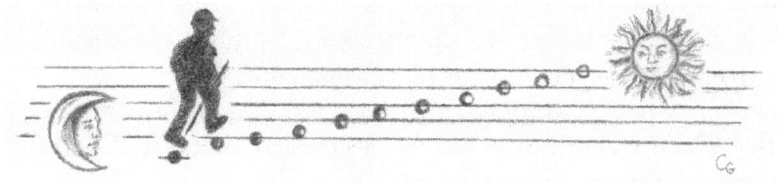

Ascending scale to Roncesvalles Abbey

Doc Faust : Tell me, is the Glory Portal still under construction as it was three years ago ? At the foot of the pier you can see the famous "Devil's Mouth". It is also called "the mouth of judgment", because pilgrims at the end of their journey placed both hands in the two openings in the column to secure a place in heaven or according to legend in hell if their hands were burned.

There we see whether or not the pilgrim has learned humility. Here we present ourselves with respect and humbleness, we lower our forehead to a few centimetres from the Holy Spirit, without ever touching it, we will never be worthy of it. We wouldn't, like the ungodly, to be struck by lightning when touching the ark of the covenant.

Mikaël : Unfortunately the Glory Gate is still under construction and we will not be able to see the blower of the "Boca del diablo". So we walked around like in any sacred monument, from left to right. We are always surprised that the priest no longer officiates in front of the altar, that the left doors of the churches are still closed, that the clams are emptied of their water !

Here too, as since the beginning of our journey in Brussels, we find this very particular Baroque style, common to many churches in the region. The nave and transepts are bare, only the choir and some chapels are loaded with exuberant decorations.

Doc Faust : Don't miss the Ascension Day Mass, it is a magical moment to share with this place.

Mikaël : We'll be there, of course ! Today we attended part of the Mass, standing near the central column of the northern transept. There are hundreds of pilgrims from all over the world attending every day. Some arrive walking, but no matter how you get there, the atmospher is more piety than elsewhere. During a liturgical chant, a strange phenomenon seized me.

To the sound of a crystalline note, I felt a door opening gently and widely at the top of my skull, then a stream of energy penetrating me and gradually filling me from head to toe.

Doc Faust : This Light that you felt is the divine spark, it is now up to you to transform it into Fire ! If you are in contact with light, it changes you very slowly. The fire will take on its new form, it is Mother Nature's laboratory. Sometimes writing is also hard work because instead of carving the stone, you refined the words.

Mikaël : Today is Ascension Day. The Cathedral of Santiago is very full and the Bishop mentioned all the groups of pilgrims, sometimes from the other side of the world. At the end of the mass, the botafumeiro, the giant 54-kilogram incense burner operated by eight tiraboleiros, flies twenty metres high between the two transepts. An expected moment, a fire that goes beyond simple folklore, not to be missed.

Doc Faust : Yes, the "Botafumeiro", purification by incense, or symbolically by fire, was originally used to purify the smells of pilgrims from all over Europe. A whole story... But I'll arrive tomorrow, it'll be easier to continue our conversations.

Together at Santiago

Doc and Mikaël in front of the horses fountain.

Doc has arrived in Santiago. The idea launched several months ago between us is now being put into practice by the side of the road. It seems so unreal to be both on the camino...

Alchemical introduction through the middle way

Mikaël : What an emotion to walk with you the last few kilometres before Santiago. I realize how lucky I am. I feel like I'm out of time. We like to walk alone on the paths, but it isn't difficult to be a lot to walk in the same path. Some pilgrims seem exhausted under their heavy burden but so happy to reach the goal of their pilgrimage.

Doc Faust : Over these last few kilometres, more and more pilgrims are coming, all walking in the same direction. Some seem luminous, while others, lost, seek to cross some glances. Also observe the bronze murals riveted to the ground, their coasts are all oriented towards Santiago, a sign that all the paths converge towards the cathedral of Santiago de Compostela. On the middle way, it's a bit the same, you bring back to yourself the energy of the world scattered all around you. Your matter will transform with the accumulation of light it receives. The appearance of the light manifested is sudden, but it requires a long process of accumulation before it can be manifested.

Mikaël : All the roads are different and yet they all lead us to the same place today, to the same quest. What a feeling to have the stick you gave me. Thank you so much for bringing them here and revealing every step of the ritual of their creation.

Doc Faust : The peregrination thus becomes quite different. The analogy I made recently between stick and sword makes sense here. After your visits to Chartres, Mount Saint Michel and recently to

Brussels together, this trip to Santiago de Compostela will be experienced, not as an outcome, but as a true WISE STEP*.

Mikaël : Despite being near of the city, the path leading to it is bucolic, look at the quantity of flowers ! The eucalyptus globulus with their starry fruits, stars as if it was raining, there is even the five-branched star of the quintessence. Also try these curious green plants called "*Venus's Navel***" !

They grow between the stones of the low walls and one cannot help but think of Sandro Botticelli's painting entitled "The Birth of Venus", the representative rising from the water standing on a scallop. It is a beautiful omen to find some here, a bit like seeing a unicorn at the bottom of the road.

Doc Faust : Yes, Venus comes out of "bitterness***", it represents the life together with the salt of philosophers, the perfect white work. You are at a crossroads as would the crusaders at Jerusalem be. You are preparing to move from the ORE to the LABORE, you will see, one never goes without the other. I would even say that without the state of consciousness in the ORE, the LABORE cannot lead you to the light manifested.

---

* In french wise step is « pas de sage », wich can be heard as « passage » : transition, gateway, passage (TN).
** Umbilicus pendulinus (TN).
*** Bitter in french is « l'amer », wich sounds like « la mer = the sea » (TN).

Alchemical introduction through the middle way

Let's get closer to the two beautiful bronze statues overlooking the valley, they represent two pilgrims contemplating the towers of the cathedral in the distance. We too are approaching Santiago.

We feel the energy concentrating in us, it will be revealed during the pilgrims' mass. So, for you there will be the Mass you lived before the path and the Mass after, it will vibrate differently.

Pilgrim statues - O Monte do Gozo (Mount of Joy) facing Santiago

Alchemical introduction through the middle way

*

Arrived at the cathedral of Santiago de Compostela. We mingle with the many bustling pilgrims who hurry to the entrance porch...

Doc Faust : We must end here, in the cathedral, the consecration of the canes. We will bathe their extremities, where the Ourobouros was carved, in the shell-shaped holy water font, because for once there is water.

Mikaël : And we will do the same with our black jet bracelets. Our jet beads are made of a local stone called azabache, pilgrims wore these stones since the Middle Ages to protect themselves from all the evil spells. For me, it is also the symbol of the black work, the passage through the little death in order to be reborn. This will help me to remember the work done, but especially the work that remains to be done.

Doc Faust : We will pass through the ambulatory, through a narrow door under the choir. Here we will discover the crypt and its tomb where the relics of the apostle James of Zebedee, known as "The Major", brother of John the Evangelist, have been placed for nearly a thousand years. An object can be put on the ground for a moment to charge it with the energies of the place.

Mikaël : We will also slip a piece of paper wrapped in the interstices of the crypt stones, a wish will be written on it.

Doc Faust. The pilgrim will put a prayer, a wish. The enlightened alchemist will be very humble and will just thank you for receiving light along the way. It is an intense moment before the demonstration. The stillness of this moment will make us unburden

Alchemical introduction through the middle way

ourselves of our inner fire and fill us with the light that comes down from heaven. The matter is open at the bottom of the crypt and the light transforms the black matter into transparent glass.

Mikaël : Let's go down into the crypt at the heart of the matter.

*

We are in a moment of recollection and immobility with, around us, a world in turmoil characterized by the flow of pilgrims who pass behind us without passing away...

In the crypt, for a moment alone, we were, a knee in the ground, during an instant liberated. As we climb up, we feel the weight of light on the void (actually the full one), at a glance we find ourselves in the place of our Offerus.

Doc Faust : Even today the cathedral is still in turmoil. During the celebration we had the pleasure of seeing the censer swinging. I felt strong vibrations in the central column of the transept, the place is powerful, the cathedral was not built here randomly.

Mikaël : Indeed, the vibration of the place is exceptional. We are receptive and in total communion with these telluric energies. Perhaps we can add to this the egregore that has developed here with the multitude of pilgrims who have passed through for a thousand years. On the bench, the vibrations were surprising because they were so powerful.

Doc Faust : Before leaving Santiago, we could visit the Pilgrimage Museum next door. It is a rich and moving place telling the story of the pilgrimage.

Fisterra, at the end of the Earth

The zero mile marker in front of the Fisterra lighthouse

We sadly left Santiago de Compostela. As it is difficult for us to leave after so many emotions, a last quick tour of the cathedral is required. We must continue because our path extends to the end of the earth.

Alchemical introduction through the middle way

Mikaël : We had the last breakfast rua da Acibecheria[ddd] at Damajuana's house just in front of the hotel, a tapas bar and restaurant generously run by Maria. This morning she gave us a piece of the famous "Tarta de Santiago", the traditional Galician cake with almond paste sprinkled with white sugar signed with the red cross of Galicia, the signs, always the signs. She didn't want to hear about payment for lunch. There are still farewells, handshakes, they are brief but meaningful, she holds us very tightly in her arms and embraces us wishing us the traditional "Buen camino" that all pilgrims exchange as they meet each other on the way.

Doc Faust : Come on, let's continue our journey, towards Fisterra, or "Finis terrae", it's the "End of the earth" but also the beginning of another one. Moreover, as for Breton Finistère, we find the same geology with granite and an exuberant flora. To increase this feeling of "déjà vu", brooms and gorse are found on the hillsides. See, over there, those beautiful pink flowers ? They are "witch claws" and the stem is made of three forked fingers. These fig-like fruits are succulent and sour. We are here in a different perception of the path, the light manifests itself around us, the light is life. All our senses are exacerbated.

Mikaël : Such amazing perfumes ! The woods and forests, mainly composed of eucalyptus, saturate our sense of smell delightfully since the beginning of our trip to Spain. This makes a significant difference with Breton Finistère.

---

ddd : Street named so because of the large number of craftsmen working on the jet (acibecheiros) and gathered in this street, in the 15th century.

Alchemical introduction through the middle way

Doc Faust : We crossed the village of Negreira, a name that cannot be invented. Have you seen the furrows, Mikaël ? How excessively black is the earth there ! Once again, we are here as in the first work. The black is a field to cultivate, a song to invent, like getting in tune with the world, aligned to receive the divine.

We now arrive in Fisterra, it is a pretty fishing port, we take the road to Cape Fisterra, to discover the "Faro". This is the real end of the road and few pilgrims go there because many stop exhausted in Santiago....

Mikaël : We will go down one end of the hillside, towards the sea, a little further than the Calvary that we see below the lighthouse, look for a gap between the rocks in order to slip a Scallop in a mural as we had done on Easter Island, and way before in Chartres Cathedral. These will stay there for a long time, we will still be connected with these shells. See Doc, we're making our way... We'll meet later for a solo espresso at the little bar near the lighthouse !

Doc Faust : So, your ritual is made again and I imagine that these scallops will merge with the landscape. Here again we feel some pretty strong vibrations, there must be huge upward energy flows.

Mikaël : You feel it too ? I didn't dare to say it, it's so amazing.

Doc Faust : Let's head for the beaches, passing by Hermedesuxo, it's a village with scattered houses. "Hermedesuxo" : another Hermès wink. All this bodes well for the future. Be careful with the signs, always the signs ! Like in Compost-stellae.

Mikaël : This is the small road so sought after, it is just as narrow as our path was, following it takes us up to the cliff.

In front of a house projected onto the solitude of the ocean, we discover the beginning of the path. This winding path aspires us towards this beautiful beach of Arnela located very far below the road...

Doc Faust : Well, here's the crescent-shaped beach, another invitation to the moon. It's the one we were looking for, it's very secluded, we're lucky. The rain and wind stop, the mist disappears and the sky turns beautifully blue. You feel the amazing contrast, a form of serenity thwarted by the violent beat of the high ocean waves, everything is predisposed to alchemy, ebb and flow, inspiration and exhalation, *solve and coagule*.

Alchemical introduction through the middle way

Mikaël : The exposure of this cove to marine currents and the incessant rolling of the waves make it easier to understand why polymetallic nodules, containing antimony ore from the ocean floor, had been harvested there for a very long time by the alchemists' apprentices.

The trail ends with a steep slope in a sand dune running away under our feet....

Mikaël : Oh ! Look in the sand at those scattered stones with bright flashes of light ! There are some very beautiful fragments of sparkling green stone, like a VITRIOL. There are also some, recorded in this ancient stratum, in a layer of silts and granitic stones that seems to have been altered by the ocean. It's an invitation to take them on a trip. Let's pick them up and study them.

Doc Faust : I've never seen things like this before. What is that supposed to be ?

Mikaël : Let's proceed step by step and observe their characters together : first of all the color, it's a deep green, it's very hard, it's quite heavy, soft to the touch, the grain is very fine, it's similar to a glass paste, let's knock two stones against each other. What do you smell, Doc ?

Doc Faust : It seems to me that it smells like sulfur.

Mikaël : You're right, it's the characteristic smell of sulfur. Look at the conchoidal breakage that reveals the volcanic glass. These breaks are mainly due to thermal differences. The monocrystalline and pasty rock on the surface of the sand is exposed to the fiery rays of the summer sun and then breaks into multiple shiny pieces under the influence of heat. Some fragments have obvious lava bubbles on their sides that once again prove the magmatic origin.

Doc Faust : Remember Mikael, these shattered fragments are like rose petals, a truth can have many facets.

Mikaël : It is most likely a green obsidian[eee], a rare stone found in Latin America. Depending on its composition and reflections, it can be called "Rainbow" or "Celestial Eye" ! ! ! ! Ours is a similar variety. We work these stones in jewellery. They are also found, polished and spherical, in esoteric shops, they are used in lithotherapy, often as protective amulets. Or, we put it under the pillow to have introspective dreams that can lead us to face the darkness of our soul... Black is black, but behind it the colors of hope are hidden.

..The blond sandy beach, which I symbolically associate with a lion trapped in a crescent moon, closes to the west by a beautiful pink granite cliff. Granite is composed of three minerals : quartz, mica and feldspar...

Mikaël : The pink of the granite is more intense here than on the Breton coast because its feldspar is richer in iron oxide. And on the right side, the cliff is cut by a deep joint. We will explore it quickly as the waves rise and it's becoming dangerous to persevere.

Doc Faust : We did not collect any nodules. It would probably be possible to discover them during high tides and after strong storms, we will have to come back... Nevertheless, the discovery of these

---

[eee] See "The Pendulum" in appendix page

stones about three hundred million years old is enough today for our joy.

Mikaël *:* Let's take a last look at this landscape after having carefully picked eucalyptus leaves. They will be subject to some extractions in the laboratory when we return.

Doc Faust *:* All these treasures play their part by taking us into an alchemical reverie. We are so happy that we could come here...

*

... The end of the journey is approaching, we return to the end of the earth, to the lighthouse of Fisterra. Once again, we go down together to the small cross, the very last one at the end of the West. The light falls, some pilgrims like us come to see, at the end of the day, the sun melting with the sea. Some goats joyfully animate the hillside and graze the grass on the cliffside. The solar star dives into the ocean like the sun in a mercury bath.

An intense emotion then overwhelms us because we have to leave and take the way back. How difficult it is to leave this place. Last year, we had spent a long time in distant islands, meeting others. During this pilgrimage to Santiago, it was another journey, an inner journey. The places were perfect for it and, like pebbles on our way, helped us to find what we had in ourselves from the beginning.

Alchemical introduction through the middle way

Mikaël : Doc, at the end of this initiatory journey, what allegory, do you think could summarize the philosophy of all our exchanges ?

Doc Faust : In the end, we could summarize all our actions with man as a pile that, connected to the universe, captures its positive and negative flows. This battery, then sufficiently charged with energy, powers a lamp that could be likened to the stone of the wise. This is how the original light goes, which is thus manifested. Man therefore benefits from an huge clarity that illuminates the shadow of nature.

Mikaël : What a beautiful image ! The path has opened a new door for us, but behind it, how many more... ?

... A sentence from Doc then resonates inside :

"The path...it is up to you to make it live in your heart".

« *Buen Camino* ! »

*

Contributors to this book :

Mikaël and Doc Faust
Many thanks to :

o for the illustrations : Christine Groult for her drawings that accompanied us throughout this trip.

o for the introductory drawing : F.B

o for corrections : A. and Ch.G.

o Michel, Companion of the Duty that gives life to our tools.

o Eleonore, for the English translation.

*Scallops with green obsidian shell from Fisterra
Work realized when we returned, by our friend Michel.*

Notes

1. Page 19 : **Salt, sulphur, mercury** - The starting material is a shapeless and dark chaos disorganized in these four elements : water, earth, air and fire. With the purification of this material, intermediate bodies appear which are the sulphur active principle (energy pushing from the inside to the outside), the salt neutral principle (which maintains the balance between energy from the inside with that from the outside) and the mercury passive principle (energy pushing from the outside to the inside).
2. Page 19 : **Fulcanelli** - Under this name was published *Le Mystère des cathédrales* (*The Mystery of the Cathedrals*) in 1926, and *Les Demeures philosophales (Dwelling of the philosophers)* in 1930. These works propose to decipher the alchemical symbolism of several monuments. As for Fulcanelli's identity, several hypothesis have been made about the person hidden under this pseudonym, perhaps a person or a group of persons writing under this name, but knowing who is behind it doesn't really matter.
3. Page 19 : **Henri Coton-Alvart** (1894-1988)
A chemical engineer, he held an important position in a research laboratory for the first part of his life and was at the origin of several discoveries in this field. He voluntarily retired from the world to devote himself entirely to philosophy and science. His passion for the

Truth led him to burn in the athanor the waste of matter and the deceptions taught, in order to open the broadest horizon to spiritual energy. Before abandoning all worldliness, he was part of the small circle in which Fulcanelli's works were born. He was friends with Pierre Dujols, Egyptologist René Schwaller de Lubicz, and poet Milosz. He met Jean-Julien Champagne, Eugène Canseliet and many painters, writers and politicians.

4. Page 19 : **Armand Barbault** (1906 - 1982)
   French chemist and alchemist. His research focused on a natural elixir: drinking gold. He tried to rework a process described in a 17th century alchemical work, the Mutus Liber. This medicine is composed of plant juices, dew and gold powder. This involves saturating plants with dew and then carrying out a complex series of cyclic distillations.

5. Page 42 : **Henri La Croix Haute** (1918-2011)
   Disciple of Henri Coton-Alvart and author of many books cited in the bibliography at the end of the book.
   To respect the author anonymity, we will not use his name but his pseudonym.

6. Page 64 : **Basile Valentin** (1565-1624)
   Under the name of Basile Valentin (in Latin Basilius Valentinus), presented as a Benedictine monk of the sixteenth century, were published at the beginning of the seventeenth century some alchemical treatises which were very successful. It turns out that these texts were written at the time of their publication, probably by their publisher, Johann Thölde.

7. Page 65 : **Universes / Bubbles** - The theory of parallel universes or multiple worlds was introduced by the American physicist Hugh Everett in 1957. It is a reinterpretation of quantum mechanics that tries to eliminate conceptual problems such as those posed by Schrödinger's cat experiment or the EPR paradox (Einstein–Podolsky–

Rosen paradox). According to this theory, Schrödinger's cat is not in an overlapping state. There are actually two cats, one living and one dead, who are part of two different universes. This is possible because when we impose the choice between a dead cat and a living cat, the Universe is divided in two. Two parallel universes are then born which are absolutely identical, except that one contains a living cat and the other a dead cat. In each of these universes, the cat is in a well-defined state and the somewhat absurd concept of an animal neither dead nor alive is no longer necessary. Finally, when we open the box and look at its contents, we select one of the two universes that then becomes our Universe. At that moment, the two parallel universes decouple and become totally independent of each other. If we discover that the cat is dead, we can be reassured by imagining that there is a parallel universe where the cat is alive. (references : internet).

8. Page 72 : **Pythagoras** - (approx. -580 to -495 BC)
The Pythagorean Tetraktys (The number 4 -Tetra and the radiant light - Actys) is represented by an equilateral triangle on side 4, each side being composed of 4 points, the triangle is constructed by 10 points. It means "four-radius". The Pythagoreans swore an oath "by the Holy Tetraktys" : "The Tetraktys in which are found the source and root of eternal nature. Everything derives from the Decade and goes back to it. The 10 is the image of the moving wholeness.

9. Page 81 : **Archetype** – "An ideal model, a supreme type or a prototype is called an archetype : in this sense, Plato's ideas are the model at the same time as the foundation of things. Many other philosophers have spoken of archetypes. However, it was the psychoanalyst Jung, Freud's dissident disciple, who spread the use of this term from 1912 onwards and gave it technical value in his psychology of the unconscious. For Jung, every individual

unconscious are rooted in a collective unconscious that is common to everyone; this unconscious encloses original types of symbolic representations, which are models of behaviour. It is these types, inherent in human nature, and psychic corollaries of biological instincts, that Jung calls archetypes. As there is, in man, a kind of a precondition of the specie on the mental plane (as are instincts on the vital plane), it is not surprising that they are found in the most different individuals, in the most distant peoples, without mutual influence. For their part, religious morphologists (Van der Leeuw, Eliade) adopt the notion of archetype to designate the fundamental symbols that serve as a matrix for series of representations. In a broad sense, the archetype is the primordial image, the mother image, the one that feeds the "personal" images and feeds them from the same "archaic" collection, which is exploited by mythologies and religions - Henry Duméry.

10. Page 90 : **Language of the birds** - According to Wikipedia, the language of the birds consists in giving a different meaning to words or a sentence, either through playing on sounds, or through word games (slang, anagrams, word fragments...), or through the use of letter symbols. The language of birds is a language coming from on cryptography, which is based on :

a) The sound correspondence of the words spoken with other silenced words allows a semantic approximation that constitutes a subtle and esoteric coding, either to mask information or to amplify the meaning of the first word.

b) The spelling, based on the mystical symbolism of the letters of the words spoken, can refer to an iconic coding that reinforces the meaning of the words, as in hieroglyphics. The oldest documents at our disposal theorizing the language of birds are by Grasset d'Orcet and Fulcanelli, (19th century). They attribute to the language of birds an immemorial origin : for a long time it would have been a language of initiates, a system of occult coding linked to alchemy and hermetic poetry. It acquires a psychological dimension in the 20th century, Carl Gustav Jung and Jacques Lacan, see in it an unconscious coding that amplifies the meaning of words and ideas. The Dictionary of Imaginary Languages lists several languages of birds. Nevertheless, there are far-fetched languages such as the language of crows without historical foundations, surely inventions of pathological cases. It is thus necessary to differentiate between "secret languages" and far-fetched languages, invented languages, jargon and dialects and imitations ("language of animals" which Mircea Eliade says consists in "imitating their cries, especially the cries of birds"). It is not forbidden to see in the expression "language of birds" an analogy with its aerial dimension since it ultimately consists in making the sound "take off", in hearing it rather than reading it. In this language where "double meaning" prevails, sound, in short, "resonates" and "reason". The analogy with birds is above all physical : sounds fly but letters remain fixed. In itself, the pun is the best way to approach the paradoxical duality of the symbol. The language of birds is therefore intimately linked to the "language of symbols". The language of birds isn't related on a specific language; in fact, each language has a similar coding system based on : lexicon, syntax, phonetics and semantics. Some authors attest, since Antiquity, to the existence of a secret language reserved for "diviums" ("diviners"), initiated into divine messages. Diodorus of Sicily, in his Historical Library, (Book V, 31) explains that there is a language of the gods : "They say, indeed, that... these men (the druids) who know the essence of the divine, so to speak, speak the same language as the gods...". Virgil in the Aeneid (Book III, 360) teaches us that the "language of birds" is one of the diviner's skills. Nevertheless, this language may have a real linguistic origin. Iambule, a Greek writer (1st century BC) in a fantastic book, writes that the inhabitants of an island in the Indian Ocean have a bifid language (cut in half) allowing two conversations to be held at the same time. There is a correspondence between Gothic art, the coded language known as slang and the myth of the Argonauts, widely evoked by alchemistic authors. This relationship could be synthesized into a sentence containing all the terms : Gothic art is a coded language used by a group of initiates to this language and looking for the philosopher's stone. Fulcanelli, in *"Les Demeures Philosophales"*, shows that the masters set in the stone of the cathedrals their ancestral knowledge, he was one of the first to clearly reveal the meaning of the birds' language. Other authors mention the language of birds : Synésios (4th century), Platon, Artéphius (12th century), Nicolas Flamel, Abbé Boudet, Richard Khaitzine...

11. Page 118 : **Paracelsus** (1493-1541)

    This Swiss doctor plays an important role in the history of medicine. He also was a philosopher and alchemist. The four pillars on which Paracelsus' medicine is based are : philosophy, astronomy, alchemy and the virtue of the doctor. In addition to these four pillars, there are three substances that make up the bodies and five entities or forces that cause disease. According to Paracelsus, any sublunar body is composed of three substances : sulphur, mercury and salt. They symbolize the body (salt), the soul (sulphur) and the spirit (mercury). Each substance is determined by its reaction to fire. Thus, sulphur represents everything that burns, mercury represents everything that evaporates and salt represents any non-combustible residue. External causes can cause reactions in each of the three substances that are hurting the balance of health. The latter therefore depends on an appropriate relationship between the three substances. For more information see *"La doctrine Spagyrique de Paracelsus"(Paracelsus spagyric doctrines*) excerpts chosen and translated by Dr. Emerit and edited by Henri Coton Alvart. Comments and notes from J-F Gibert.

12. Page 130 : **EST- NON – EST (Be – Not- Be)** - Shield of faith, the Scutum Fidei, "shield" or "emblem" of faith is a traditional symbol in Western Christianity. The first known representation is from the very beginning of the 13th century. This shield is named after the epistle 6 of Saint Paul to the Ephesians "Put at your feet the zeal that the Gospel of peace give; take above all this the shield of faith, with which you can extinguish all the fiery features of the evil one; take also the helmet of salvation, and the sword of the Spirit, which is the word of God".

13. Page 205 : **Hermes** - In Greek mythology, Hermes is one of the deities of Olympus, he is the messenger of the gods. Hermes is likened to Thut, the Egyptian god of hidden knowledge. His name was later borrowed under the name of Thrice-Great Hermes, or Hermes Trismegistus, to whom some mythical writings were attributed. These will form the basis of a true esoteric library, which will then feed the work of the alchemists of the Middle Ages. His name evolved according to cults and cultures : Hermes, Mercury, then his cult spread until he became Michael, and finally Saint Michael. Mikael being the anagram of Alkemia.

14. Page 227 : **Easter Island** - As early as the 12th century (or even much earlier) King Hotu Matua's tribe left the Marquesas Islands to colonize a new land (165 km^2, wich is about 64 square miles) signalled by scouts on the return from a long and perilous exploratory journey of several thousand kilometres. Polynesians used to build "Marae" temples, but also "Tikis" stone sculptures. On Easter Island, the 887 moai (invariable term) carved for the majority between 1250 and 1500 were moved over long distances and on very irregular ground, then erected on "Ahu" temples. It required exceptional technique, resources

and power to transport these statues, which were 2.5 to 9 m high and weigh an average of 14 metric ton (and one of 80 metric ton which was not extracted from the quarry). In 1998, a member of the Atan family told us that mana was essential to move the moai. In addition, our team, on the sides of a vertiginous cliff, discovered in 1983, in a cave until then unexplored but used as a shelter for a rat, 800-year-old nuts from a variety of endemic and disappeared palm trees (palm tree that we called Paschalocos disperta (y*ou can learn more about that on wikipedia*). This discovery made it possible to close the debate following the observation of a strain at the foot of an ahu by J.L. Palmer in 1868 and to definitively determine the pollens collected from the lake of the Rano Kau crater by J. Flenley in 1979. Our friend Jean Dausset (Nobel Prize for Medicine 1980) took blood samples from the Pacific Islands for genetic analysis, the results allowed him to certify the Polynesian origin of pascuans, but later contacts with Latin America are not excluded.

15. Page 264 : **Saint Christopher** - According to legend, Christopher was called, before his conversion, Offerus. He was a five-metre-high giant who went from king to king in order to serve the greatest king in the world. From disillusionment to disillusionment, a surveyor entrusted him with the mission of helping travellers cross a river with the help of a tree transformed into a cane.

Alchemical introduction through the middle way

Appendices

Table of planetary correspondences (p. 68)

	Elements / Microcosm				Principles			Celestial spheres				The creator
	Fire △	Earth ▽̄	Water ▽	Air △̄	Sulphur	Salt ⊕	Mercury ☿	Sulphur Wise ♃	Sun ☉	Mercury ☿	Moon ☽	Light ✡
Alchemical Planets	Mars ♂	Saturne ♄	Venus ♀	Jupiter ♃	Sulphur		Mercury		Sun	Mercury	Moon	Chrysopée / Macrocosm
Virtues — Cardinal	Strength	Precaution	Temperance	Justice	Faith		Charity	Intelligence			Wisdom	
Theological / Tarot Blades	XI	XII	X	IX	XIX		XVIII	I			II	XXI
Polarity	Male	Female	Female	Male	Male		Female	Male			Female	Dual
Metals	Iron	Lead	Copper	Tin	Gold		Silver	Gold			Silver	Celestial rebis
Day of the week	Tuesday	Saturday	Wednesday	Friday	Sunday		Monday	Thursday				
Deities — Greece	Hades / Ares	Cronos	Aphrodite	Zeus	Apollon		Artemis	Hermès				
Rome					Phébus		Diane	Mercure				
Babylonian	Nergal	Minurta	Ishtar	Marduk	Sin		Shamash	Nabû				
Colors — Harrakhians	Red	Grey	White	Orange	Yellow		Blue	Iridescent				
Alchemical (Mylius)	Red	Black	Blue	Green	Yellow		White	Hope	Brown			
Alchemical (Classic)	Red	Brown	Blue	Blue			Silver	Spiritus	Silver	Silver	Green	
Orientation — Astrology	South	Green	Green	Blue				Neutral				
Hermetic	Southeast	North	West	East	Southwest		Northeast					
Livings — Folleville												
Nantes François II	Mark	Luke	Matthew	John	Peter		Jacques				John Baptist	
Tetramorph — Christian	Lion	Bull	Man	Eagle								
Bestiary — Alchemical (Mylius)											Queen	Hermaphrodite

317

Alchemical introduction through the middle way

- Echelle de Bovis (p. 202)

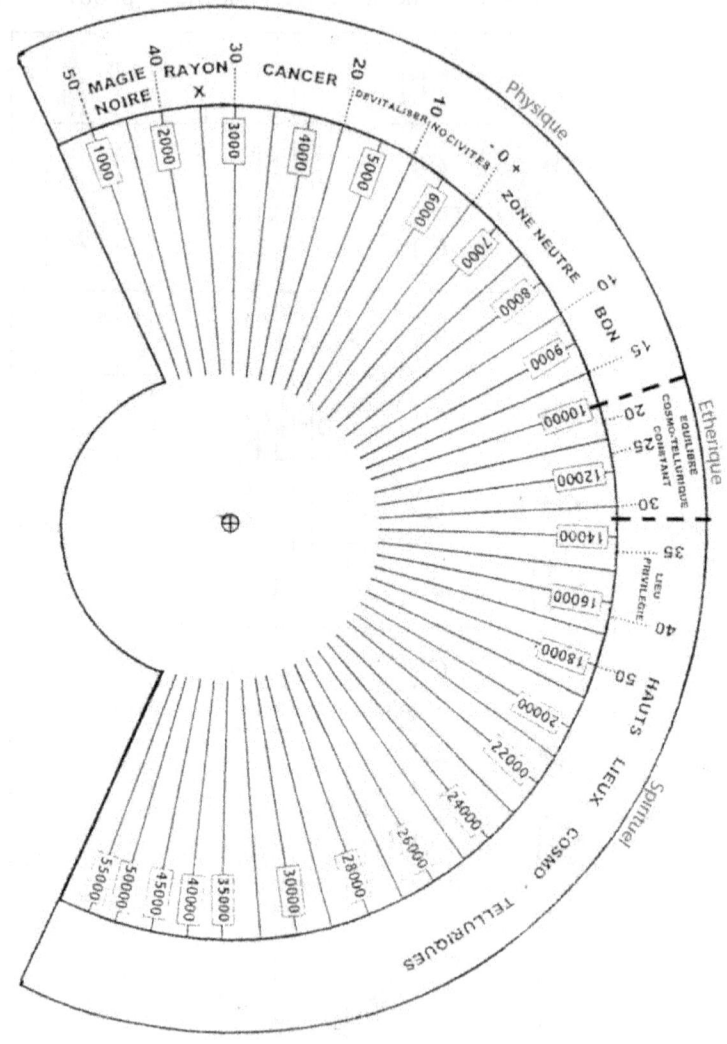

318

○   A unique Pendulum (p.306)

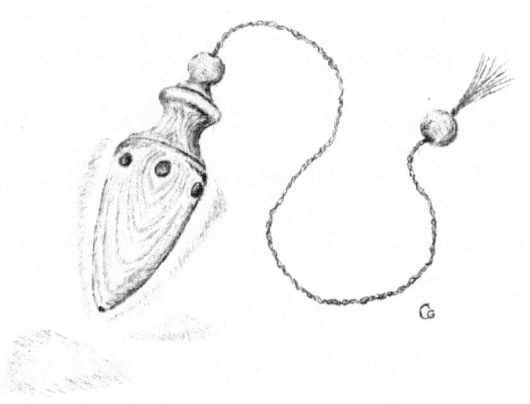

The pendulum is said to be the extension of the hand, like the continuity of the range of our energy field. We had the happy surprise of receiving from our friend Michel, a pendulum designed with great art, made of boxwood. It is decorated with green stones, you know the obsidian found in Fisterra, we gave him one of these stones when we returned from Compostela. This pendulum was made for Pernelle according to tradition with sacred proportions : 3-6-9 (three levels, six set stones, the inlay holes drilled from side to side forming a six-pointed star, the cord is braided with nine horsehair). The assembly is carried out with the propolis from his bees. Its dimensions also have a meaning. In order to protect it, a tiny iron point is plugged into its end. Finally, it was consecrated in a high place... This extraordinary pendulum has a very special feature: held vertically by its cord, it vibrates particularly and when it turns a beautiful coloured aura mysteriously envelops it.

Reading suggestion in a certain order

> **Editions Philomène – Alchimie**
> (available books by www.editionsphilomenealchimie.com)

Philomène, Philosophe par le feu, *Entrée alchimique par la voie du milieu*, éd. 2017.

MA de Nantes, *Clef des œuvres de saint Jean et de Michel de NostreDame*, version complétée et annotée avec index, éd. 2019.

Anonyme (1865), *La clef du laboratoire hermétique*, éd. 2019.

Philomene, Philosopher by fire, *Alchemical introduction by the middle way*, éd. 2019.

Jean-Marie Groult & Yves Fostier, « *Rouen symbolique - Rouen alchimique* », éd. 2019.

Jacques Hylae, *Hélisthène*, éd. 2019.

Sabine Stuart de Chevalier, *Discours philosophique sur les trois principes* (en 3 vol.), version traduite en français usuel, complétée et annotée avec index, éd. 2020.

Jean-Marie Groult & Yves Fostier, *Folleville symbolique - Folleville alchimique*, éd. 2020.

Yves Fostier, Christian Attard et Jean-Marie Groult, *Abbaye de Saint-Amand-les-Eaux historique et alchimique*, éd. 2020.

Véronique Cauchy-François, *La Fontaine aux étoiles*, éd. 2020.

Richard Khaitzine, *Secrets d'Alcôves, Fulcanelli et la cosmosphère* (en 2 vol.), éd. 2020.

Jacques Hylae, *Contes du Feu de Dieu*, éd. 2020.

M.A. de Nantes, *Résurrection merveilleuse en 1877 de M. de NostreDame mort en 1566*, version complétée et annotée avec index, éd. 2021.

Christian Attard, *Hôtel de Pierre, une demeure philosophale à Toulouse*, éd. 2021.

Didier Rabosée, *de l'Argile à la Pierre, l'initiation alchimique de Thomas le potier*, éd. 2021.

Blaise de Vigenère, *Traité du Feu et du Sel*, version traduite en français usuel, complétée et annotée avec index, éd. 2021.

Raimon Arola, *Le Symbole Renouvelé*, traduction de Jeanne d'Hooghvorst, éd. 2021.

Richard Khaitzine, *Peter Pan, symbolisme et hermétisme des contes de fées*, éd. 2021.

Richard Khaitzine, *Le Petit Chaperon Rouge, symbolisme et hermétisme des contes de fées*, éd. 2021.

Richard Khaitzine, *Le Chat Botté, symbolisme et hermétisme des contes de fées*, éd. 2021.

> **The classics :**

Marcellin Berthelot – *How to become an alchemist.*
Albert Poisson – *Theory and symbols of alchemists.*
Fulcanelli – *The mystery of cathedrals (for the good wheat without the chaff).*
Fulcanelli – *Dwelling of the Philosophers (for the good wheat without the chaff).*
Eyrénée Philalethe - *The marrow of alchemy - Volumes I, II and III.*
Altus – *Mutus Liber.*
Cyliani – *Hermes unveiled.*
Salomon Trismosin – *The Splendor Solis.*
Basile Valentin – *The Twelve Keys to Philosophy.*
Sabine Stuart le Chevalier – *Philosophical speech.*
Blaise de Vigenère –*Treatise of fire and salt.*

> Some classics from the RETZ collection Bibliotheca Hermetica

Nicola Flamel - *The book of hieroglyphic figures.*
Le Cosmopolite - *New chymic light to clarify the three principles of Nature.*
Limojon de Saint Didier - *The Hermetic Triumph.*
Dom Pernety (Antoine-Joseph) - *Hermetics Myths dictionary.*
Eyréné Philalethe - *The open entrance to the king's closed palace.*
Basile Valentin - *The last will.*
Basile Valentin - *The triumphant cart of antimony.*

➢ The out of categories

Henri Coton-Alvart - *The two Lights.*
Nicolas Lémery - *Chemistry course - New edition 1757.*
Eugène Viollet Leduc - *Encyclopedia of the Middle Ages.*
Henri La Croix-Haute :
- *Alchemist's Bestiary.*
- *Body, Soul, Spirit, by a philosopher.*
- *Astrological correlations*
- *Philosophicals tales.*
- *As the days go by.*
- *Philosophical meditations*
- *About the « Two Lights »*
- *The Heliotrope manuscript.*

➢ Furnace works far away from the middle way :

Armand Barbault - *The gold of the thousandth morning*
Atorène - *The alchemical laboratory*
Eugène Canseliet - *The alchemy on its classical writtings.*
Jean Laplace - Rudimentum Alchimiae.
Jean Pascal Percheron - *The golden book of alchemy.*
Loïc Trehedel - *Alchemy, antique science of the future.*
Pierre Dujols and Henri Coton-Alvart - *The Labora-T-ore.*
Solazaref - *The hermetical sum.*

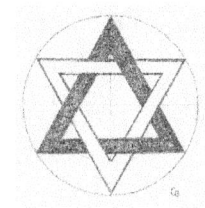

Illustration table

F.B - Introductory drawing of the page 8

D.F - Pictures and illustrations of the page : 32, 34, 73, 91, 101, 102, 103, 104, 125, 136, 162, 273, 296, 317.

Christine Groult - Drawings of the pages : 14, 18, 23, 27, 33, 35, 37, 47, 51, 60, 63, 68, 75, 77, 78, 85, 88, 93, 109, 111, 113, 117, 120, 131, 133, 138, 141, 147, 157, 160, 163, 172, 177, 180, 185, 197, 200, 204, 207, 213, 215, 219, 227, 231, 245, 256, 260, 263, 265, 269, 284, 289, 293, 299, 302, 309, 319, 321, 325, 329.

M - Pictures and illustrations of the page : 1ère de couverture, 56, 61, 97, 127, 132, 151, 183, 259, 287, 308.

Various archives - pages : 71, 106, 257, 318.

All rights reserved ©

Contents

Foreword by Voyageur	....	p. 9
Introduction	....	p. 15
The begining of the teaching	....	p. 23
The Adepthood	....	p. 27
Fulcanelli's Myth	....	p. 39
We must be silent	....	p. 47
Sacred symbolism's	....	p. 51
The alchemical Laboratory	....	p. 63
The Tetraktys	....	p. 71
We are interconnected	....	p. 77
A surveyor on the path	....	p. 85
Light and Philosopher's Stone	....	p. 93
Universe or Multiverse	....	p. 109
The Alkahest	....	p. 117
The cardinal virtues	....	p. 127
The wonder	....	p. 133
Transmission	....	p. 141
The metamorphosis	....	p. 151
The Ginkgo elixir	....	p. 163
Ora and Labora	....	p. 177
Stanza… on the way	....	p. 187
Be aware of signes	....	p. 197
Listening is art	....	p. 207
Symbolic connexion	....	p. 213
From black to white	....	p. 219
The initiatory journey	....	p. 227
Connexity with Easter Island	....	p. 231
Back to the laboratory	....	p. 245

Morning dew	....	p. 259
Pilgrimage to Santiago de Compostella	....	p. 269
The craftsman and the alchemist	....	p. 273
On the camino frances	....	p. 287
Together at Santiago	....	p. 293
Fisterra at the end of the Earth	....	p. 299
Contributors	....	p. 307
Endnotes	....	p. 309
Appendix	....	p. 317
Reading suggestions	....	p. 321
Illustration table	....	p. 325
Table of content	....	p. 327

Tous droits réservés ©

Imprimé en France par Jouve

733 rue Saint-Léonard 53100 Mayenne

N° d'imprimeur : 878587559

Dépôt légal : janvier 2017

www.ingramcontent.com/pod-product-compliance
Lightning Source LLC
Chambersburg PA
CBHW050125170426
43197CB00011B/1721